# The Debt Term-O-Nator

by John Avanzini

HIS Publishing Company
Fort Worth, Texas

*The Debt Term-O-Nator*
ISBN 1-878605-13-5

1997 Edition

*The Debt Term-O-Nator* is a revised version of the book,
*Rapid Debt-Reduction Strategies,* published by HIS
Publishing Company in 1990 with over 350,000 copies in
print.

**HIS Publishing Company**
**P.O. Box 917001**
**Ft. Worth, Texas 76117-9001**

# Contents

*I dedicate this book to*
*Michael and Nancy Davis,*
*faithful partners to this ministry.*

# Foreword

Nothing makes the devil happier than binding God's children hand and foot in financial bondage. He knows we are entering harvest time, the time when the fields of humanity are ripe.

We now have the ability to reach the nations as never before. Even with the tremendous inflation of this world's currency, it is more economical to reach the multitude of lost souls than it has ever been. Christian television is, without a doubt, God's end-time tool of mass evangelism. We can literally touch billions of souls for a fraction of the cost of reaching only a small portion of the world a few decades ago. However, we still have one major obstacle to overcome. I speak of the chains of debt that hang heavily upon God's children.

For years it seemed as if nothing could be done about it. Then God started revealing to His servants that He was willing to go farther than canceling their sin debt. He would also cancel their financial debt.

Yes, God cares about the every-day bills His children owe—the house payments, car payments, second mortgages, even the small loans and credit card debts. Every financial trap that catches His dear children is of great importance to Him. It is exactly as the psalmist so graphically stated. **"Surely [our God] shall deliver thee from the snare of the fowler. . ."** (Psalm 91:3). There can be no question about it. He is a debt-canceling God, and one of His favorite end-time miracles is canceling the debts of His dear children.

There is also a practical side to getting out of debt. There are strategies, or better said, "witty inventions" for quickly paying off debts. That is exactly what this wonderful book by John Avanzini contains. You will find strategies for rapidly paying off mortgages, automobile loans, and a really quick way to pay off credit card debt.

The title of the book, *The Debt Term-O-Nator*, really says it all, for if you follow its simple steps, debt termination quickly follows.

You now have the book in your hand. Hold onto it. Use it. Its strategies have worked for others, and they will work for you.

*Paul Crouch, President*
*Trinity Broadcasting Network*

# Special Notice

*The information in this book is in accordance with the following statement:*

This book is intended to provide you with lay advice on ways and means of overcoming debt and is not intended as a substitute for **sound legal and accounting advice** from your attorney or financial advisor.

These are procedural suggestions, **not specific directions.** Before acting on any of these suggestions, you should thoroughly check what has been written to determine the proper course of action you should take. No two financial situations are exactly alike. **Always seek professional counsel before making changes in your financial matters.**

Anything you attempt to do toward the rapid reduction of any loan must be in agreement with that loan's legal document. The lender, as well as the borrower, has the right to reject any procedure that is not specified in the loan agreement.

The information in this book is, to the author's knowledge, conceptually correct. The mathematics used in the amortization schedules are based on standard mathematical formulas. The exact numbers may vary slightly from other amortization schedules due to the manner in which numbers are rounded. There may also be a difference due to the way the interest is calculated. (Some loans are figured on a 365-day year while others are figured on a 360-day year.)

Please remember there are hundreds of possible combinations of interest, principal amounts, and contractual agreements which may make it impossible to apply everything in this book to all loans. The examples herein are given only to illustrate the concepts explained. Even if they seem to fit your particular circumstances, your lending agreement and attorney's advice will supersede any suggestion made.

If your loan agreement contains anything not in accordance with federal, state, or local laws, neither this publication, its author, nor its owners will seek remedy for you or provide you with advice concerning relief. If your loan company will not allow you to operate any of the strategies in this book, neither this publication, its author, nor its owners will attempt to dissuade them or speak to them on your behalf. Your accountant or attorney should be contacted in such matters at your own expense.

# Introduction

## You Now Have a Plan

If you don't have an out-of-debt plan, rest assured you are under the influence of someone else's into-debt plan. If you don't learn anything else from this book, I want you to realize that **any time money is involved, nothing just happens by itself.** There is always a strategy at work, one that will either force money into your hands or force money out of your hands. If you are to be successful in the realm of finance, **you need a well-formed plan to keep you out of debt's control.**

No matter how bad your finances might be—no matter how hopeless things seem—rest in the knowledge that **you now have a plan available to you.** It is a plan that has successfully helped folks much like you to get out of debt. From this day on you no longer have to be a clay pigeon in the shooting gallery of debt. You are about to learn a special plan and a group of strategies which can make you debt free and give you financial independence.

## Credit Comes of Age

In the last thirty years, the credit industry has come into full maturity. No longer is it just a convenience made available to those who cannot pay cash. It is a full-grown, multi-billion dollar industry which **sells its services** as a part of **every financial transaction** you enter. Apparently, multiplied billions of dollars are being spent annually by the credit industry to project the **illusion** that the easy-payment plan is helping the population into a better lifestyle. It is high time we **wake up** and examine whether or not that is true.

## No Holds Barred

Each and every day the unrelenting devourer called "interest" is eating a **bigger bite out of every dollar** you spend. It seems the "easy-payment industry" is taking every possible advantage available **to keep you permanently in as much debt as you can possibly pay.** Make no mistake about it. **It is not a coincidence that you cannot seem to get out of debt.** It appears to be the result of a well-executed plan.

If your credit rating is good, new strategies are apparently being devised **to get you deeper into debt.** Once you are in to your limit, they seem to work to **keep you there for the rest of your life.** If you are to survive this relentless attack against your assets, you must **fight back with a master plan of your own.** I don't mean a plan that will just get you out of debt. I am speaking of a plan that **will get you out and keep you out.** It's time for you to declare all-out **war on debt!**

The master plan in this book **is not an experiment.** This plan has been proven time and again. It has worked in my life as well as in the lives of others. When my wife and I faithfully executed it, this plan rapidly took us from the depths of debt into **the completely debt-free lifestyle** we now enjoy.

## Buried in Debt

When I say we were in debt, believe me, **we were buried in it.** Even the experts said our case was hopeless. The only advice anyone gave us about our financial situation was to **immediately file bankruptcy.**

As unbelievable as it seems today, **the master plan** in this book quickly brought us out of debt. Our payout took place so rapidly that some of **our most skeptical creditors** actually asked us to explain to them **how we were able to make such a rapid recovery** from such an overwhelming debt load.

## Our Knowledge Was Limited

When we came out of debt the first time, we didn't understand it was possible to live without owing money on our automobile, home, or big-ticket items. I am ashamed of what I must now confess, but in the years that followed, we **drifted right back into the bondage of debt.** We accumulated loans on the television, appliances, second mortgages, credit cards, and so on. **It wasn't long until we were once again up to our eyeballs in debt!**

At this time, we realized that without a plan to **stay out of the grip of debt,** we would continually fall back into it.

The second time we approached our debt payoff, we made up our minds to become **totally debt free.** To accomplish this plan, we realized we would have to **change our basic mentality.** If we didn't, we would have no way to **keep from being trapped by debt again.**

## It's Not Wrong to Borrow

Please note that I don't believe in **never borrowing.** In a time of need, **a properly handled loan** can serve you well. However, there is **a special philosophy** you must apply to any loan which you take **if that loan is not to rule you!** You must be determined not to live a lifestyle of debt.

## This Time the Mortgage Would Go

The second time we rapidly paid our way out of debt, we had some new artillery, for we had discovered some things about mortgages that I wonder if **the lenders wanted us to know.** Not only am I curious as to whether they wanted us to know, I would like to hear how they feel about my letting you know. We found there were some **strategic ways of paying a mortgage** that automatically cut many years off the loan. Not only were years cut off, but in the process, we were able to **save thousands, even tens of thousands of dollars** off the actual cash outlay called for in our thirty-year loan.

## This Time Car Notes Would Also Go

We also learned a strategy which made it possible for us to purchase the very best of automobiles on a 90 to 120-day loan instead of paying for them over a five-year period. **Sometimes we are even able to pay cash on delivery.**

In this book, all these strategies are made available to you. As you read it, realize that some consultants are charging hundreds, and even thousands of dollars to help people in matters such as these. I believe as you read, you will find **answers** to your own debt dilemma.

## You Can Do It

**Don't be afraid** that you won't be able to do it. It is easier **when you know how.** Remember, it was someone else's into-debt strategies that brought you into your present financial mess. Now **your own out-of-debt strategy** is available to help you rapidly get yourself out of that mess. **There is always help for those who try to help themselves.**

# 1

# Know Where You Are

It is impossible to navigate an airplane to a predetermined destination unless **you know where you are.** It doesn't matter how advanced your navigational equipment might be. If you cannot determine **your present position,** it will be difficult to reach **a desired destination.**

## Make Two Lists

The same principle is true when it comes to getting out of debt. You need two points of reference. First, you must know **exactly how much you owe.** Second, you must know **exactly how much you own.**

In this chapter, you will find two example lists. One is titled, **"How Much I Owe."** The other is titled, **"Things I Own."** Because of the limited page size in this book, it will be necessary for you to construct your own lists using these examples as models. Fill them out as completely and accurately as possible.

When you have completed them, they will help you understand more clearly your present financial position. With this information in hand, you can begin to more easily manage your finances in a way that will serve your best interests. The importance of these lists will become more evident as you proceed.

# Know What You Owe

To find out your starting point, complete the **"How Much I Owe"** list first. I am sure **this will be the most painful part of the entire process** of getting out of debt. It will take some real strength and dedication to your purpose to face the truth. You will probably want to kick yourself when you see some of the foolish things you have allowed the spirit of debt to influence you to do.

## Don't Leave Anything Out

Be sure to list every bill. **Each one is important.** Any debt you omit will make **your position weaker** and **your debt's position stronger.** List each bill, its due date, the interest rate, the dollar amount of each payment, and the remaining balance. You should also list the number of payments left for each item.

*Example*—**"How Much I Owe" List**

| Bill Owed | Orig. Amt. | Int. Rate | Bal. | # Pmts. Left | Payoff Date |
|-----------|-----------|-----------|------|--------------|-------------|

## What Should Really Count

Don't be too rough on yourself if you don't like what you discover. What should really count is that **you are doing something about your debt** situation. Keep reminding yourself that what you are doing is **not a temporary, stop-gap measure.** It will lead to **a permanent solution.**

As you look at the growing list of what you owe, you may think there is no use going any further. Please don't let that type of thinking stop you. If you do, this book cannot help you. **Take my word for it.** If you continue, you will be

glad you did. No matter how painful it is, you must continue until all your debts are listed.

Remember, you cannot reach your destination of debt freedom unless you know your starting point. Before you can begin your rapid debt-reduction program, you must know how much debt you have to eliminate.

## Know What You Own

If you are like most people, you have accumulated many things over the years. When your **"Things I Own"** list is completed, **it may well surprise you** to see how many things you actually own. When your possessions are scattered around the house, yard, and neighborhood, it is difficult to understand just what you have.

As you make your list, be thorough.* The more exact you are, **the more powerful your war on debt will be.**

*Example*—**"Things I Own" List**

(Check "Not" if item is not needed. Check "Need" if item is needed. Check "Want" if item is not needed, but wanted.)

| Item | Cost | Loan | Not | Need | Want | Value | Sell |
|------|------|------|-----|------|------|-------|------|

## Use It or Sell It

Now **you must make an important decision** about each item you listed. You must decide whether or not you will need

---

*       *The Victory Book* contains many ready-made forms to help you formulate your out-of-debt plan. To order, see the catalog in the back of this book.

it. Be assured, this is not just an incidental question. It is a very important part of your accelerated out-of-debt strategy.

You should also decide which items you don't need but **would like to keep.** These items should be clearly distinguished from the items **you don't want to keep.** With this information, you can now begin to intelligently build a list of **the things you will sell.**

## Not Everything Can Be Sold

Pay close attention to the items on which you still owe money. It is important that you thoroughly read your loan agreement. Before you try to sell anything which still has money owing, you must be sure there is no restriction which forbids selling it before it is paid off. There may also be other peculiarities that call for a different approach. If you have any questions about whether or not something can be sold, ask the lender and check with your attorney.

## Be Rational

Don't get caught up in the spirit of selling and **mistakenly part with something you really need.** You must be even more careful when considering things you don't need but would like to keep. Use your good judgment to be sure you **don't mistakenly sell something which might end up being one of your primary forms of enjoyment during the time you are getting out debt.**

For instance, a bicycle you no longer use may be a lot of fun when **credit-card-financed entertainment** is no longer available. You may not be using a certain piece of exercise equipment now. However, it might be much more useful to you in the months ahead. It might just help you let off some steam.

## Simple Test

A simple test for determining if an item should be kept or sold is listed below:

1. Do I really want to sell the item?

2. Will I enjoy having the item more than I will enjoy paying off the portion of debt its sale would accomplish?

3. Will the item become of greater value to me during the months ahead?

With this simple, three-step test, you should be able to easily make quality decisions as to what you should keep and what you should sell.

Now begin to make the list of things you will sell. Remember, the money you raise from their sale will be used to make a major pay down of the debts you now owe.

# 2
# The Master Plan Strategy

It is now time to explain what I call **"the master plan."**
This plan is the miracle my wife and I discovered during the
late 1960s. It was the time in our lives when it seemed
absolutely impossible for us ever to get all our bills paid.

We owed huge amounts of money. Our debt included **a
number of major credit cards,** every one of them charged
to the limit. At least three cards had balances over $10,000.
Besides the credit card debt, we owed **several signature
loans to banks.**

Our **numerous gasoline credit cards** had long since
been canceled, leaving enormous unpaid balances. Every one
of our **department store cards** was at its maximum allowed
limit. Payments on several **loans from individuals** were in
delinquency. Our **previous year's income tax** payment was
six months overdue. Both of our new **automobiles had been
repossessed.** We lost our three **homes through foreclosure.**

## Bankruptcy Seemed Our Only Hope

To say our situation was bad would be a great
understatement. **It was impossible!** We were no longer able
to even maintain a home for our five children. **We lived with
my father and mother.**

With this **mountain of debt towering over us,** we were
faced with the heaviest of decisions. **Should we take
bankruptcy,** as most people were advising, or **should we**

**somehow try to dig our way out** of this avalanche of unpaid bills? If we chose to pay our way out, **it would take years.** All of our plans would have to be put on hold. We would face the dismal task of doing nothing more than **paying bills for the next six to ten years.**

I must admit that **bankruptcy seemed to be our only hope.** We had lived under financial pressure for so long that **our thinking process had become flawed.** We had come to the point of no longer seeing ourselves ever being debt free again. Neither could we bear the thought of facing the mountain of bills which were systematically **destroying our joy as well as our marriage.** We were living exactly as the Bible says:

> **. . . the borrower is servant to the lender.**
> **Proverbs 22:7**

As I look back, I am so thankful for the revelation of the master plan. It was so wonderful to get control of our debts and begin to pay them off that I made up my mind one day I would help others become debt free. Now that I am able to do so, **I present to you the master plan.** I hope it brings you the joy it gave to my loved ones and me.

## I Was Addicted to Credit

I finally realized my problem. I was **hopelessly addicted to credit buying.** I was being held captive under the power of debt. It was not until I broke that compulsion that I was able to successfully put these plans to work.*

---

\*   *War On Debt* explains how to break the power of credit addiction. To order, see the catalog in the back of this book.

On the eve of making our decision whether or not to take bankruptcy, I said to my wife, "Pat, let me spend **one last night with these bills** and see if there isn't some way to get them paid off."

That night I made many calculations. I looked at my bills from every conceivable angle. Then, all of a sudden, **the master plan was revealed to me.** It came as a **complete surprise.** When I saw it, I was amazed that I had never thought of it before. Not only had I never thought of it, I had never even heard of it before. The plan is **so simple,** yet **so powerful.** When I showed it to my wife the next morning, **she immediately confirmed that it would work.**

## The Golden Rule

Before I explain this plan, I want to share an important biblical principle that will **move your out-of-debt program beyond your own abilities.** No doubt you are familiar with *the golden rule.*

> **. . . all things whatsoever ye would that men should do to you, do ye even so to them: for this is the law and the prophets.**
> **Matthew 7:12**

Whatever you cause to happen for someone else, **God will cause that same thing to happen for you.** Scripture is clear about it. You will reap what you sow.

> **. . . whatsoever a man soweth, that shall he also reap.**
> **Galatians 6:7**

Getting out of debt is no exception to this rule. If you help someone else get out of debt, **God will be faithful in**

**helping you get out of debt.** Read what the Word of God says:

> . . . whatsoever good thing any man doeth,
> the same shall he receive of the Lord. . . .
> **Ephesians 6:8**

## A Revolutionary Thought

Hold on to your hat, for I am about to share a revolutionary thought with you—one that will enable you to **help someone else pay off his debts.**

You may be saying, "Wait a minute! I thought *I* was going to get out of debt!" You are, but remember what you just read. Whatever you cause to happen for someone else, God will cause that same thing to happen for you! You can actually **recruit the help of Jehovah God** in getting yourself out of debt if you will help someone else out of debt.

## The Choice Is Yours

Whoever you choose to help is up to you. You may want to help one of your children, another relative, your church, or your favorite Christian television station. As you choose who you will bless with a seed toward their debt reduction, you will open the doorway through which **God can bring your own miracle of debt cancellation.** With every seed you plant, you establish the biblical basis for God to help speed you out of your debt problem.

According to the principles of biblical economics, you can **reach financial freedom more quickly if you help someone else reach financial freedom.**

# Your Church Is a Good Place

I suggest you earnestly consider starting an out-of-debt campaign in your own local church. Wouldn't it be exciting to have your entire church family getting out of debt while they are paying the church corporation out of debt at the same time?**

Even if your church as a whole doesn't participate, you can still plant your out-of-debt seed there. Simply follow this plan on your own. When it is time for you to plant a seed, designate it for "Church Debt Reduction," and give it to your church.

You may choose someone else or some ministry other than your local church in which to plant your out-of-debt seed. With each seed you plant, simply send a note explaining that the recipients are to apply the amount given to the payoff of their debts. (Just be sure you are planting in good ground.)

# Keep the Windows Open

For this plan to be the most effective, **you should be a faithful tither** to your local church. If you are not tithing, the Bible says you are robbing God.

> **Will a man rob God? Yet ye have robbed me. But ye say, Wherein have we robbed thee? In tithes and offerings.**
> **Malachi 3:8**

---

** For more details on this plan, see *The Victory Book*. To order use the catalog in the back of this book.

The Bible goes on to say **the windows of heaven are not open over the lives of non-tithers.** If you have never committed yourself to be a tither, please do so immediately.

## The Plan

As I now begin to explain what was revealed to me that night, please **pay very close attention.** At first it may seem **too simple to work on such a complex problem** as the one you face. However, if you will give it an honest try, I am confident it will bring you **out of debt in quick order.**

Just open your mind, follow with me, and see how much sense this plan makes.

## One Big Bill

Your first step in taking dominion over your bills is to stop looking at them as if they are many bills. From this day forward, you must look at them as if they are combined into **one, giant bill.**

Now don't let the thought of one big bill throw you. **It is not as bad as it sounds.** Granted, you will now be dealing with your bills as if they are one giant bill, but you will also do the same with your many payments.

## One Big Payment

From this day forward you must consider that you have **one great, big payment** to make on that big bill. This giant payment will consist of the total amount of all your present payments added together.

Now here is the power behind this plan. While your **big bill will become less** each time one of the smaller bills is paid off, your **big payment will stay the same** until the last bill is paid in full. Do you see how special this makes your one, big payment? It will become **more powerful each time one of your bills is paid off,** for it will then be able to do more toward paying off your remaining debt.

Step by step, with the payoff of each bill, you will be able to eliminate more and more of your debt with your one big payment. At some point in time, it may even **seem that your payment has doubled,** or even tripled in value. I can hear you ask the question, "How can this be?"

For illustration purposes, let's say you owe a total of $20,000 on your combined bills. If you continue to pay them at the minimum allowable payments each month, it is obvious that you will spend many years making payments on them before they are all paid.

Let's say your payments total up to $1,400 per month. Suppose this amount is made up of twenty bills ranging in payments from $7.50 per month to a car note of $220 per month. None of them pay off on the same date. You may still owe sixty payments on one, fourteen payments on another, and maybe only three more payments on yet another one.

Remember, you must make your new, giant payment of $1,400 **faithfully each and every month until every last bill is paid in full.** Yes, you read right. When a bill is paid off, the monthly payment **does not, I repeat, does not go down.**

# Targeted for Destruction

Now focus on the bill which will be paid in full in only three months. Suppose its payment is $80. Remember! When this bill is paid, you are **not** going to have an extra $80 to spend. Instead you are going to have **$80 extra to apply to the next bill** you target for destruction.

Now pay close attention. The next bill scheduled for destruction will not necessarily be the one with the least number of payments remaining. You must **target the bill with the highest monthly payment** that the extra $80 per month will pay off the **fastest.**

# Think Before You Act

Clear thinking is important at this point. Suppose you have a bill that will be paid off in three months if you apply your extra $80 to it. If that bill has a payment of $75 per month, **it may not be the best one to pay off next.** It would be better to use your extra $80 on a bill with **a higher monthly payment,** even though it may take **a little longer to pay.**

For example, if you have a bill with a $125 monthly payment which is close to being paid off, add your extra $80 to that bill each month. **Even if it takes an extra month or two** to pay it off, it is worth waiting in order to have an additional $125 every month to apply toward other bills.

The reason behind this is easy to understand. If you pay off the $75 monthly bill, you will have only $155 extra each month ($80 + $75) to apply against the next bill. However, if you pay off the $125 a month bill, you will have $205 extra each month ($80 + $125) to use toward your next bill.

## Pay Off the Car in Only a Few Months

During the final months of your master plan payoff, you will be paying bills off in one month that would have taken as long as a year at the minimum payments. There will also be a day when you can apply the entire $1,400 per month to your automobile loan. This will allow you to pay off the car in only a few months instead of the remaining three or four years which the regular payment would have taken.

## Pay Off the House Next

When the entire $1,400 is available, why not take four or five hundred dollars for your regular monthly spending; then apply the extra $900 to $1,000 each month to your home mortgage. Why, in just a few more years, *you will really be debt free.*

# 3

# Powerful Mortgage-Payment Strategies

It would take most people the greater part of their lives to save enough money to pay cash for a home. When you consider this fact in conjunction with the ever-increasing cost of houses, it becomes evident that you should accomplish home ownership as soon as possible, **even if you must borrow to do it.**

## You Can Have a Debt-Free Home

The person who desires to buy a home but must use monthly payments, can now safely do so. The time-payment purchase of a home no longer has to take thirty years. I say this because many borrowing **strategies are no longer a secret.** With the discovery of these strategies, **the informed borrower now has an advantage.**

If you approach your mortgage with the strict resolve of **paying it off as soon as possible,** you can save many years and thousands of dollars off the traditional thirty-year home loan. The key ingredient in **taking control of your mortgage** is an unswerving determination that you will, **under no circumstances,** take thirty years to pay it off. To do this you must **employ one or more of these effective strategies.**

You must make additional pay downs for any rapid debt-reduction strategy to work. While there is no strategy that will lower the principal amount you borrow, there are a number of ways to **drastically lower the interest costs** which the lender will be legally entitled to collect from you.

## The Mathematical Advantage

There are **powerful mathematical facts** you, the home buyer, can now know about mortgages. The following strategies are **mathematically sound methods** which can greatly reduce the **expense, as well as the time** it takes to pay off your home loan. Each strategy is **conceptually correct.** However, it is your responsibility to get the lending institution which holds your loan to agree to any modifications made to your present loan agreement. Remember, your mortgage holder is not obligated to do anything not expressly stated in the loan agreement you signed.

Do not become discouraged at this statement. If your mortgage does not expressly forbid prepayment, 90 percent of the obstacles are already out of the way. I am sure you can make some, if not all of the following rapid-payoff strategies work for you.

## If the Bank Says No

If your banker rejects your rapid-payoff plan, **don't give up.** It's not necessarily over. There still may be something you can do. First, find out if your present loan has any form of prepayment restriction. This may be wording that says **you cannot pay off the principal in advance,** or it may state that **a payoff penalty will be charged if you do so.** In many states it is now illegal for a  lender to refuse a home owner the right to prepay his mortgage.

# Be Courteous

Courteously ask your loan officer if you can begin prepaying the principal due on your mortgage. Give him an opportunity to agree. However, if he says no, thank him and leave. But **do not give up hope.** Try one more thing before contacting your state's banking authority for help. Just as if you had never said anything, go right ahead with your plan for a rapid payoff. Mail in your payment as you always do, enclosing the regular monthly amount, plus any additional amount you wish to prepay on the principal balance.

# Write One Check

When you make your payment, **do not write two checks.** Add any extra amount you wish to pay on your loan to the check you would normally send. It has been reported that these payments are almost never refused by the bookkeeping departments of lending institutions. They usually just apply the extra payment to the principal without any further discussion.

# Keep Good Records

Warning! Once you begin a rapid debt-reduction strategy, always check that your entire regular payment and **all of your prepayments** have been accepted and **properly credited to your account.** It is absolutely necessary that you keep a file of the canceled checks for all payments you make. Always attach the receipt to the check. Begin your file on the date you first make a prepayment until your loan is paid in full. Always insist that the bookkeeping department of your lending institution provide you a **correct balance with each month's receipt.** Check that this new balance includes a deduction of your prepayment for that month.

31

It is very important that **every payment you make be properly recorded.** Your canceled check, coupled with your lender's monthly statement **showing your pay down** should be sufficient evidence of payment. Do not make the mistake of keeping only a copy of each check you write. You must also **keep the original check,** for the lender's **endorsement will appear on the back** of each one. This is proof that they accepted your payment.

# 4

# The First-Day Payment Strategy

Let's begin with one of the most powerful prepayment strategies in existence. It is an amazing way to quickly reduce the balance on your mortgage while also greatly reducing the time it takes to pay it off.

To get the greatest benefit from this strategy you must make the first payment on your loan **the day it is activated.** By this I mean the first payment must be made **on the day the lender begins to charge interest** on the money you are borrowing. If you use this method, an unbelievable **number of months will automatically be deducted** from the full term of your loan. In some cases your thirty-year mortgage can be **shortened by more than four years.** Think of it. All of that savings is yours by simply making one payment in advance. Keep in mind that the exact amount of savings **fluctuates with the interest rate** and term that apply to each mortgage.

## An Example

In the case of a $100,000 mortgage with an interest rate of 14.5 percent, you will deduct four years and six months from the term of the loan by this simple strategy. This thirty-year mortgage will be automatically reduced to twenty-five and a half years. You can actually save four and a half years of payments (54 months) **by making only one payment at the right time.** This payment will also cause a great interest savings. In the case of a $100,000 mortgage at this rate, the interest savings will be $64,900.48.

This strategy works so well because during the first years of your mortgage only a small part of each monthly payment is applied to lowering your principal balance. With the $100,000 mortgage example, if the first payment is made on the due date, only $16.23 of the $1,224.56 payment is used to pay off the balance. This means that **a whopping $1,208.33 of that first payment goes toward interest.** However, if the first payment of $1,224.56 is made before any interest is charged, the full amount of the payment goes toward paying off your $100,000 balance.

Now see some amazing facts about the savings this strategy makes on the above-mentioned mortgage. You would have to pay the $1,224.56 payment for **a full twelve years and eight months** before even $100 of each payment would be applied to your mortgage balance. Keep this in mind. If you pay according to the thirty-year plan, the major portion of every payment will be paying interest **for almost the entire life of your mortgage.** Your only hope of saving money comes from the amount of interest you can eliminate by prepaying the principal.

## Not Necessarily a First-Payment Strategy

This strategy will never accomplish more drastic results than it does with the first payment. However, you can apply it at any time during the life of your mortgage. Whenever it is applied, it will always bring big results.

I have projected this plan in several different ways at the end of this chapter. By these comparisons you will be able to see what a substantial difference is made in a loan by making one, two, three, four, or five payments on the day the loan is made. With each additional payment you are able to make on the first day, your mortgage is more drastically shortened.

## Give a Really Big Gift to Your Children

This strategy is a great way for parents to give their children a really big annuity. Using a $100,000 mortgage at 14.5 percent interest, if you **make only five payments** for your children on the day they borrow the money, your gift will cost $6,122.80. However, you will actually be giving them **a gift worth $168,947.76.** This is the amount of **interest they will never have to pay** on that loan. And that's not all. You will **shorten their thirty-year mortgage by eleven years and nine months.** That means their thirty-year mortgage will automatically become a nineteen-year, three-month mortgage. Just think of how nice this gift would be for a loved one!

When you begin to use this first-day payment strategy, **you take control of your mortgage.** Keep in mind that after you have applied this strategy, you can still **apply one or more of the other strategies** from the following chapters to pay off your loan even more rapidly.

## Say No to the Loan Officer

It has been brought to my attention that when some people try to execute this strategy, they meet resistance. The loan officer tries to tell them they cannot pay any payments on the day they borrow the money. After some insistence, some loan officers reluctantly suggest the borrower just borrow a smaller amount. For instance, if the loan is $100,000 and the payment is $1,224.56, they suggest making the mortgage $98,776 ($100,000 - 1,224 = $98,776).

Don't be fooled. This is not a rapid debt-reduction strategy. The loan of $98,776 will still take thirty years to pay. It will save you less than $100 a month from your payment.

Remember, **you must have a reduction of years and interest cost** from your loan to have a true rapid-debt reduction strategy. To borrow $1,224 less only saves you $1,224 in principal. To pay down a $100,000 loan on day one with a $1,224.56 prepayment saves you four and a half years of payments (54 payments) and $64,900.48 in interest. **Don't be rude, but just say no** if the loan officer tries to get you off course.

# Support Information
# The First-Day Payment Strategy
# 12% Interest Rate

Loan Amount . . . . . $100,000.00
Term . . . . . . . . . . 30 Years
Payment . . . . . . . $1,028.61

| PMT # | PMT AMT | MOS SAVED | YRS SAVED | INTEREST SAVED | YRS TO PAYOFF |
|-------|---------|-----------|-----------|----------------|---------------|
| 1 | 1,028.61 | 31 | 2yrs 7mos | 30,853.14 | 27yrs 5mos |
| 2 | 2,057.22 | 54 | 4yrs 6mos | 53,509.55 | 25yrs 6mos |
| 3 | 3,085.83 | 74 | 6yrs 2mos | 73,003.58 | 23yrs 10mos |
| 4 | 4,114.44 | 90 | 7yrs 6mos | 88,430.22 | 22yrs 6mos |
| 5 | 5,143.05 | 103 | 8yrs 5mos | 100,834.68 | 21yrs 6mos |

This illustration shows what will happen when 1 through 5 payments are made before any interest is due. This strategy also works on existing mortgages.

## The First-Day Payment Strategy
12% Interest Continued

| PMT AMT | PRIN | PMT # | INT | BAL | TOTAL INT |
|---|---|---|---|---|---|
| 1,028.61 | 28.61 | 1 | 1,000.00 | 99,971.39 | |
| 1,028.61 | 28.90 | 2 | 999.71 | 99,942.49 | 1,999.71 |
| 1,028.61 | 29.19 | 3 | 999.42 | 99,913.30 | 2,999.14 |
| *Payments 4 through 29 omitted to conserve space.* | | | | | |
| 1,028.61 | 38.18 | 30 | 990.43 | 99,004.71 | 29,863.09 |
| **One First-Day Payment** | | | | | |
| 1,028.61 | 38.57 | 31 | 990.05 | 98,966.15 | 30,853.14 |
| 1,028.61 | 38.95 | 32 | 989.66 | 98,927.20 | 31,842.80 |
| *Payments 33 through 52 omitted to conserve space.* | | | | | |
| 1,028.61 | 48.00 | 53 | 980.61 | 98,012.95 | 52,529.42 |
| **Two First-Day Payments** | | | | | |
| 1,028.61 | 48.48 | 54 | 980.13 | 97,964.47 | 53,509.55 |
| 1,028.61 | 48.97 | 55 | 979.64 | 97,915.50 | 54,489.19 |
| *Payments 56 through 72 omitted to conserve space.* | | | | | |
| 1,028.61 | 58.57 | 73 | 970.04 | 96,945.40 | 72,034.12 |
| **Three First-Day Payments** | | | | | |
| 1,028.61 | 59.16 | 74 | 969.45 | 96,886.25 | 73,003.58 |
| 1,028.61 | 59.75 | 75 | 968.86 | 96,826.50 | 73,972.44 |
| *Payments 76 through 88 omitted to conserve space.* | | | | | |
| 1,028.61 | 68.68 | 89 | 959.93 | 95,924.45 | 87,470.97 |
| **Four First-Day Payments** | | | | | |
| 1,028.61 | 69.37 | 90 | 959.24 | 95,855.09 | 88,430.22 |
| 1,028.61 | 70.06 | 91 | 958.55 | 95,785.02 | 89,388.77 |
| *Payments 92 through 101 omitted to conserve space.* | | | | | |
| 1,028.61 | 78.17 | 102 | 950.45 | 94,966.53 | 99,885.01 |
| **Five First-Day Payments** | | | | | |
| 1,028.61 | 78.95 | 103 | 949.67 | 94,887.58 | 100,834.68 |
| 1,028.61 | 79.74 | 104 | 948.88 | 94,807.84 | 101,783.55 |

This illustration shows the effect of 1 through 5 first-day payments on a standard amortization schedule. The boxed number is how many payments are eliminated by making the first-day payment. The underlined number is the balance after making the first-day payment. The circled number is the interest saved.

# Support Information
# The First-Day Payment Strategy
# 10% Interest Rate

Loan Amount . . . . . $100,000.00
Term . . . . . . . . . . 30 Years
Payment . . . . . . . . $877.57

| PMT # | PMT AMT | MOS SAVED | YRS SAVED | INTEREST SAVED | YRS TO PAYOFF |
|---|---|---|---|---|---|
| 1 | 877.57 | 18 | 1yr 6mos | 14,941.01 | 28yrs 6mos |
| 2 | 1,755.14 | 34 | 2yrs 10mos | 28,106.89 | 27yrs 2mos |
| 3 | 2,632.71 | 49 | 4yrs 1mo | 40,337.34 | 25yrs 11mos |
| 4 | 3,510.28 | 61 | 5yrs 1mo | 50,033.40 | 24yrs 11mos |
| 5 | 4,387.85 | 73 | 6yrs 1mo | 59,642.05 | 23yrs 11mos |

This illustration shows what will happen when 1 through 5 payments are made before any interest is due. This strategy also works on existing mortgages.

**The First-Day Payment Strategy**
10% Interest Continued

| PMT AMT | PRIN | PMT # | INT | BAL | TOTAL INT |
|---|---|---|---|---|---|
| 877.57 | 44.24 | 1 | 833.33 | 99,955.76 | |
| 877.57 | 44.61 | 2 | 832.96 | 99,911.15 | 1,666.30 |
| 877.57 | 44.98 | 3 | 832.59 | 99,866.18 | 2,498.89 |
| *Payments 4 through 16 omitted to conserve space.* | | | | | |
| 877.57 | 50.52 | 17 | 827.05 | 99,195.66 | 14,114.38 |
| **One First-Day Payment** | | | | | |
| 877.57 | 50.94 | 18 | 826.63 | 99,144.72 | 14,941.01 |
| 877.57 | 51.37 | 19 | 826.21 | 99,093.36 | 15,767.22 |
| *Payments 20 through 32 omitted to conserve space.* | | | | | |
| 877.57 | 57.69 | 33 | 819.88 | 98,327.63 | 27,287.49 |
| **Two First-Day Payments** | | | | | |
| 877.57 | 58.17 | 34 | 819.40 | 98,269.45 | 28,106.89 |
| 877.57 | 58.66 | 35 | 818.91 | 98,210.79 | 28,925.80 |
| *Payments 36 through 47 omitted to conserve space.* | | | | | |
| 877.57 | 65.34 | 48 | 812.23 | 97,402.22 | 39,525.66 |
| **Three First-Day Payments** | | | | | |
| 877.57 | 65.89 | 49 | 811.69 | 97,336.33 | 40,337.34 |
| 877.57 | 66.44 | 50 | 811.14 | 97,269.90 | 41,148.48 |
| *Payments 51 through 59 omitted to conserve space.* | | | | | |
| 877.57 | 72.18 | 60 | 805.39 | 96,574.32 | 49,228.61 |
| **Four First-Day Payments** | | | | | |
| 877.57 | 72.79 | 61 | 804.79 | 96,501.53 | 50,033.40 |
| 877.57 | 73.39 | 62 | 804.18 | 96,428.14 | 50,837.58 |
| *Payments 63 through 71 omitted to conserve space.* | | | | | |
| 877.57 | 79.74 | 72 | 797.83 | 95,659.73 | 58,844.88 |
| **Five First-Day Payments** | | | | | |
| 877.57 | 80.41 | 73 | 797.16 | 95,579.32 | 59,642.05 |
| 877.57 | 81.08 | 74 | 796.49 | 95,498.24 | 60,438.54 |

This illustration shows the effect of 1 through 5 first-day payments on a standard amortization schedule. The boxed number is how many payments are eliminated by making the first-day payment. The underlined number is the balance after making the first-day payment. The circled number is the interest saved.

# Support Information
# The First-Day Payment Strategy
# 8% Interest Rate

Loan Amount . . . . . $100,000.00
Term . . . . . . . . . . 30 Years
Payment . . . . . . . . . $733.76

| PMT # | PMT AMT | MOS SAVED | YRS SAVED | INTEREST SAVED | YRS TO PAYOFF |
|---|---|---|---|---|---|
| 1 | 733.76 | 11 | | 7,308.23 | 29yrs 1mo |
| 2 | 1,467.52 | 20 | 1yr 8mos | 13,244.84 | 28yrs 3mos |
| 3 | 2,201.28 | 30 | 2yrs 6mos | 19,792.74 | 27yrs 6mos |
| 4 | 2,935.04 | 39 | 3yrs 3mos | 25,639.57 | 26yrs 10mos |
| 5 | 3,668.80 | 47 | 3yrs 11mos | 30,797.67 | 26yrs 1mo |

This illustration shows what will happen when 1 through 5 payments are made before any interest is due. This strategy also works on existing mortgages.

41

## The First-Day Payment Strategy
8% Interest Continued

| PMT AMT | PRIN | PMT # | INT | BAL | TOTAL INT |
|---|---|---|---|---|---|
| 733.76 | 67.10 | 1 | 666.67 | 99,932.90 | |
| 733.76 | 67.55 | 2 | 666.22 | 99,865.36 | 1,332.89 |
| 733.76 | 68.00 | 3 | 665.77 | 99,797.36 | 1,998.66 |
| *Payments 4 through 9 omitted to conserve space.* | | | | | |
| 733.76 | 71.23 | 10 | 662.53 | 99,308.53 | 6,646.18 |
| **One First-Day Payment** | | | | | |
| 733.76 | 71.71 | 11 | 662.06 | 99,236.82 | 7,308.23 |
| 733.76 | 72.19 | 12 | 661.58 | 99,164.64 | 7,969.81 |
| *Payments 13 through 18 omitted to conserve space.* | | | | | |
| 733.76 | 75.62 | 19 | 658.14 | 98,645.64 | 12,587.21 |
| **Two First-Day Payments** | | | | | |
| 733.76 | 76.13 | 20 | 657.64 | 98,569.55 | 13,244.84 |
| 733.76 | 76.63 | 21 | 657.13 | 98,492.92 | 13,901.97 |
| *Payments 22 through 28 omitted to conserve space.* | | | | | |
| 733.76 | 80.82 | 29 | 652.95 | 97,861.16 | 19,140.34 |
| **Three First-Day Payments** | | | | | |
| 733.76 | 81.36 | 30 | 652.41 | 97,779.81 | 19,792.74 |
| 733.76 | 81.90 | 31 | 651.87 | 97,697.91 | 20,444.61 |
| *Payments 32 through 37 omitted to conserve space.* | | | | | |
| 733.76 | 85.80 | 38 | 647.97 | 97,109.12 | 24,992.17 |
| **Four First-Day Payments** | | | | | |
| 733.76 | 86.37 | 39 | 647.39 | 97,022.75 | 25,639.57 |
| 733.76 | 86.95 | 40 | 646.81 | 96,935.80 | 26,286.39 |
| *Payments 41 through 45 omitted to conserve space.* | | | | | |
| 733.76 | 90.48 | 46 | 643.28 | 96,401.82 | 30,154.99 |
| **Five First-Day Payments** | | | | | |
| 733.76 | 91.09 | 47 | 642.68 | 96,310.73 | 30,797.67 |
| 733.76 | 91.69 | 48 | 642.07 | 96,219.04 | 31,439.74 |

This illustration shows the effect of 1 through 5 first-day payments on a standard amortization schedule. The boxed number is how many payments are eliminated by making the first-day payment. The underlined number is the balance after making the first-day payment. The circled number is the interest saved.

# 5

# The Split-Payment Strategy

Another explosive way to rapidly pay off a mortgage is to make **half payments every fourteen days.** Pay close attention to what I just said. I did not say you must make half payments twice a month; I said you must make a **half payment every two weeks** (fourteen days).

The power behind this strategy is twofold. Following this plan will cause you to automatically make **one extra payment every year.** You will also be lowering the principal balance of your loan twenty-six times instead of the standard twelve times per year. This may seem too simple for it to do much good, but the effect it will have on your mortgage is most impressive. This simple plan can quickly **take a substantial number of years off the term of your loan.** It will also save you many thousands of dollars in interest.

## How It Works

This is how it works. As you know, there are fifty-two weeks in each year. If a half payment is made every two weeks, **you will make twenty-six half payments each year.** Figure it out. Twenty-six half payments are equal to **thirteen whole payments.** If you pay one full payment each month, you will make only twelve payments each year. Also, with the split-payment schedule, you will be making a pay down on the balance of your note every fourteen days. This means you will be paying interest on a rapidly decreasing principal amount. These two factors reduce your mortgage every fourteen days instead of every thirty days, and make an important **extra payment each and every year.**

## A Bit More Each Month

In actuality you will be paying a bit more each month than you would if you made twelve regular monthly payments. However, the additional amount you will be paying is **insignificant when compared to the tremendous amount you will save.** On a $500 monthly payment, the extra cost is only $9.62 per week.

## Don't Be Stopped

If for some reason your lender refuses to let you pay every two weeks, **do not give up on this strategy.** You might still be able to operate it **without his express permission.** Here is how that is done. Instead of making your regular payment of $500, add a prepayment amount of $41.67 to your regular payment each month. That will make your total payment $541.67. If you notice, this is still the same amount that your average monthly overpayment would be if you were making your payment every two weeks.

Forcing this strategy is dependent upon there being no prepayment restriction on your mortgage. If there is a penalty, you should read it carefully. Many times this is charged only on the amount that is prepaid, not on the entire amount of the unpaid balance. In the case of the illustration, the pay down is $41.67 per month. If you had even as much as a 5 percent prepayment penalty, this strategy would still be profitable. Five percent of $41.67 is only $2.08. You would just add that amount to the payment and stipulate that it is the 5 percent penalty on your prepayment that month.

# You Can Figure It Out

You can easily figure the amount you will have to add to your own house payment in order to follow this strategy. Simply divide the amount of your regular monthly payment (payment only, not escrow costs) by twelve and add that amount to each of your regular monthly payments. This extra amount will total one extra payment each year. This will give you almost the same advantage you would have if you made half payments every two weeks.

# An Example

Using the model thirty-year mortgage of $100,000 at 14.5 percent interest, if this mortgage is paid with the split-payment strategy, **it will save $174,697.75** in interest. It will also **reduce the amount of time** it will take to pay off this mortgage **by thirteen years, and three months.** This means that by applying this strategy, you will **turn your thirty-year mortgage into a sixteen-year, three-month mortgage.** Notice this is almost down to half of the original term of the loan.

At the end of this chapter I have compared the regular monthly-payment mortgage with the split-payment strategy. I have carried the plan through to payoff using interest rates of 12, 10, and 8 percent.

# Support Information
# The Split-Payment Strategy
# 12% Interest Rate

### 30-Year Comparison

| | Monthly Payment Amount $1,028.61 | | Split-Payment Amount $514.31 | |
|---|---|---|---|---|
| **YR** | **BAL** | **INT** | **BAL** | **INT** |
| 1 | 99,637.12 | 11,980.47 | 98,486.40 | 12,372.67 |
| 2 | 99,228.22 | 11,934.45 | 96,772.43 | 12,172.29 |
| 3 | 98,767.46 | 11,882.59 | 94,831.54 | 11,945.38 |
| 4 | 98,248.26 | 11,824.15 | 92,633.70 | 11,688.43 |
| *Years 5 through 13 omitted to conserve space.* | | | | |
| 14 | 87,636.58 | 10,629.80 | 46,255.92 | 6,266.38 |
| 15 | 85,705.71 | 10,412.48 | 37,627.25 | 5,257.60 |
| 16 | 83,529.96 | 10,167.60 | 27,856.25 | 4,115.27 |
| 17 | 81,078.27 | 9,891.66 | 16,791.69 | 2,821.71 |
| 18 | 78,315.64 | 9,580.72 | 4,262.31 | 1,356.89 |
| 19 | 75,202.64 | 9,230.35 | 0.00 | 93.97 |
| 20 | 71,694.83 | 8,835.55 | | |
| 21 | 67,742.15 | 8,390.67 | | |
| 22 | 63,288.17 | 7,889.37 | | |
| 23 | 58,269.31 | 7,324.49 | | |
| 24 | 52,613.94 | 6,687.98 | With this strategy, | |
| 25 | 46,241.32 | 5,970.73 | you will never have to | |
| 26 | 39,060.49 | 5,162.53 | make any of these | |
| 27 | 30,968.96 | 4,251.82 | payments! | |
| 28 | 21,851.22 | 3,225.61 | | |
| 29 | 11,577.11 | 2,069.25 | | |
| 30 | 0.00 | 766.24 | | |
| | | $270,300.52 | | $154,309.14 |

## Savings with this strategy:
## Interest—$115,991.39   Time—11 yrs

# Support Information
# The Split-Payment Strategy
# 10% Interest Rate

### 30-Year Comparison

| YR | Monthly Payment Amount $877.57 | | Split-Payment Amount $438.79 | |
|---|---|---|---|---|
| | **BAL** | **INT** | **BAL** | **INT** |
| 1 | 99,444.12 | 9,974.98 | 98,461.87 | 10,309.09 |
| 2 | 98,830.04 | 9,916.77 | 96,755.76 | 10,141.11 |
| 3 | 98,151.65 | 9,852.47 | 94,863.33 | 9,954.79 |
| 4 | 97,402.22 | 9,781.43 | 92,764.24 | 9,748.12 |
| *Years 5 through 13 omitted to conserve space.* | | | | |
| 14 | 83,905.72 | 8,502.13 | 53,977.78 | 5,929.34 |
| 15 | 81,664.56 | 8,289.70 | 47,413.62 | 5,283.06 |
| 16 | 79,188.72 | 8,055.02 | 40,132.59 | 4,566.19 |
| 17 | 76,453.63 | 7,795.77 | 32,056.41 | 3,771.04 |
| 18 | 73,432.14 | 7,509.37 | 23,098.25 | 2,889.05 |
| 19 | 70,094.26 | 7,192.98 | 13,161.77 | 1,910.74 |
| 20 | 66,406.86 | 6,843.46 | 2,569.05 | 867.82 |
| 21 | 62,333.34 | 6,457.34 | 0.00 | <u>34.41</u> |
| 22 | 57,833.27 | 6,030.79 | | |
| 23 | 52,861.99 | 5,559.57 | | |
| 24 | 47,370.14 | 5,039.01 | | |
| 25 | 41,303.23 | 4,463.95 | With this strategy, | |
| 26 | 34,601.03 | 3,828.66 | you will never have | |
| 27 | 27,197.03 | 3,126.85 | to make any of these | |
| 28 | 19,017.73 | 2,351.56 | payments! | |
| 29 | 9,981.95 | 1,495.08 | | |
| 30 | 0.00 | <u>548.91</u> | | |
| | | **$215,925.77** | | **$139,109.00** |

## Savings with this Strategy:
## Interest—$76,816.77      Time—9 yrs 11 mos

# Support Information
# The Split-Payment Strategy
# 8% Interest Rate

30-Year Comparison

| | Monthly Payment Amount $733.76 | | Split-Payment Amount $366.88 | |
|---|---|---|---|---|
| YR | BAL | INT | BAL | INT |
| 1 | 99,164.64 | 7,969.81 | 98,336.28 | 8,242.10 |
| 2 | 98,259.94 | 7,900.48 | 96,528.66 | 8,098.21 |
| 3 | 97,280.15 | 7,825.39 | 94,564.71 | 7,941.87 |
| 4 | 96,219.04 | 7,744.06 | 92,430.91 | 7,772.02 |
| *Years 5 through 13 omitted to conserve space.* | | | | |
| 14 | 79,332.33 | 6,449.89 | 57,793.53 | 5,014.80 |
| 15 | 76,781.56 | 6,254.40 | 52,479.50 | 4,591.79 |
| 16 | 74,019.08 | 6,042.69 | 46,705.88 | 4,132.20 |
| 17 | 71,027.31 | 5,813.41 | 40,432.92 | 3,632.86 |
| 18 | 67,787.23 | 5,565.09 | 33,617.43 | 3,090.33 |
| 19 | 64,278.22 | 5,296.17 | 26,212.49 | 2,500.88 |
| 20 | 60,477.96 | 5,004.92 | 18,477.15 | 1,885.13 |
| 21 | 56,362.29 | 4,689.50 | 9,762.77 | 1,191.45 |
| 22 | 51,905.02 | 4,347.90 | 294.72 | 437.77 |
| 23 | 47,077.79 | 3,977.95 | 0.00 | .91 |
| 24 | 41,849.91 | 3,577.29 | | |
| 25 | 36,188.12 | 3,143.38 | | |
| 26 | 30,056.40 | 2,673.46 | **With this strategy, you will never have to make any of these payments!** | |
| 27 | 23,415.75 | 2,164.53 | | |
| 28 | 16,223.93 | 1,613.36 | | |
| 29 | 8,435.20 | 1,016.44 | | |
| 30 | 0.00 | 369.98 | | |
| | | **$164,155.25** | | **$117,856.82** |

# Savings with this strategy:

## Interest—$46,298.43     Time—7 yrs 2 mos

# 6

# The Specified Principal-Prepayment Strategy

This strategy is one of those things which sounds absolutely impossible when you first hear of it. **By simply adding a specified amount** to your mortgage payment each month, you can remove one payment from the term of your loan. This strategy allows you to operate your home loan as if it were a high-yield **personal investment program.**

## Amortization Schedule Required

For this strategy, **you will need to have an amortization schedule** of your loan. It must show you the two things you need to know to operate this method successfully. You will have to know exactly how much of each payment is being expended for the previous month's interest, and you will need to know exactly how much will be applied to the principal of your loan the following month.

Upon examination of your amortization schedule, you will see that the interest cost during the first two-thirds of your loan takes **almost the entire amount of each monthly payment.** Also note that with each payment, the interest cost goes down a few cents, and the principal payment goes up that same amount. For the greater part of a thirty-year mortgage, the amount that goes toward the principal remains low.

# Pay $180,265 to Pay Off $7,000

Using our model $100,000 thirty-year mortgage at 14.5 percent interest, it takes twelve years and eight months of payments before the lender begins to apply a full $100 per month to the principal of your loan. It will take seventeen years and seven months before $200 per month is applied against the balance. This is the most discouraging aspect of a thirty-year loan. When you realize that you will pay $180,265.82 on a $100,000, 14.5 percent note before a full $100 per month begins to be applied to your principal, it is enough to make you sick all over.

Now pay attention and let the next statement sink in. After paying $180,265.82, you still owe $92,908.76 on the original $100,000 you borrowed. During the first thirteen years of this mortgage, it will cost you an unbelievable average of $26,590 for each $1,000 you pay on the principal balance of this loan.

## Don't Get Discouraged

Don't get discouraged. There is something you should know about that pitifully small amount which goes against your principal during the first two-thirds of your mortgage. **This is the secret.** If you simply add the amount of next month's principal payment to this month's regular payment, **one whole payment will automatically be canceled from your loan.** That's right! It is canceled and you will never have to pay it!

## Example

Let's use our model thirty-year mortgage of $100,000 at 14.5 percent interest. The payment is $1,224.56. On the example at the end of this chapter, you will see that the amount which goes toward interest the first month is $1,208.33. (See illustration #1.) The amount going toward your loan payoff is a measly $16.22. Now look at the amount that will go toward the principal next month. It is just $16.42. If you add this $16.42 to your first regular payment, **you will never have to make payment #2** on your loan! Increase your first payment by this small amount, and you can skip payment #2. (Don't misunderstand. For this strategy to work, **you must make a payment every month until the loan is paid in full!**) The interest amount of that payment is permanently deducted from your mortgage. I say again; it will never have to be paid.

Notice that **by investing only $16.42 in your home mortgage,** you have made $1,208.14 in savings on the total cost of your home loan. This is why I call it a personal investment program. Every time you make a principal payment in advance, the next payment can automatically be skipped, and that whole month's interest cost will be saved.

Please note that if you repeat this strategy when you make payment #3 the following month, you should add $16.82, the principal amount of payment #4. Add this amount to payment #3, and the fourth payment will never have to be paid. If you operate this strategy the first two months, you will be saving $2,415.88 in interest as well as taking two months off the length of your mortgage. Your balance will not be that of a mortgage with two payments made. It will be the balance of a mortgage with four payments made.

## Let's Speed It Up

Now let's speed up the process. If you are able to spend just a little more each month, you can really shorten your payoff time. If, when payment #1 is due, you are able to add just $49.86 to your payment, you will be able to skip payments #2, #3, and #4. (See illustration #2.) They will be eliminated by paying their principal amounts. This means that when the second month's payment becomes due, you will make payment #5, not payment #2. What you have done is to make four principal payments at once, bypassing payments #2, #3, and #4. With this move you have saved $3,623.82. That is a great return on only a $49.86 investment. Besides that, **you have also chopped three months off your mortgage.**

Now let's really **turn up the heat.** Let's say that when payment #1 is due, you have an extra $173.41 to invest. With this amount added to payment #1, you can eliminate payments #2 through #11. (See illustration #3.) The interest savings will be a whopping $12,072.15. You have accomplished this with only a $173.41 investment in your mortgage. Very few investments can make this kind of money.

Now that you know this prepayment secret, you can **save a bundle** on your mortgage. Why, you might even end up rich!

# Support Information
# The Specified Principal-Prepayment Strategy
# 14.5% Interest Rate

### Illustration 1
**Making One Principal Payment in Advance**

Loan Amount . . . . . . . . . . . . . $100,000.00
Term . . . . . . . . . . . . . . . . . . 30 Years
Total Regular Interest . . . . . . . . . $340,840.13
Total Regular Interest & Principal . . . $440,840.13

| PMT AMT | PRIN | PMT # | INT | REG BAL |
|---|---|---|---|---|
| 1,224.56 | 16.22 | 1 | 1,208.33 | 99,983.78 |
| 1,224.56 | (16.42)* | 2 | 1,208.14 | 99,967.36** |
| 1,224.56 | 16.62 | 3 | 1,207.94 | 99,950.74 |
| 1,224.56 | 16.82 | 4 | 1,207.74 | 99,933.92 |
| 1,224.56 | 17.02 | 5 | 1,207.53 | 99,916.90 |
| *Payments 6 through 9 omitted to conserve space.* | | | | |
| 1,224.56 | 18.07 | 10 | 1,206.48 | 99,828.66 |
| 1,224.56 | 18.29 | 11 | 1,206.26 | 99,810.37 |
| 1,224.56 | 18.51 | 12 | 1,206.04 | 99,791.86 |
| 1,224.56 | 18.74 | 13 | 1,205.82 | 99,773.12 |
| 1,224.56 | 18.96 | 14 | 1,205.59 | 99,754.15 |

*Principal Prepayment
**New Balance

*If one principal prepayment is made every month,*
## Savings with this strategy:
## Interest—$170,119.79   Time—15 yrs.

# Support Information
# The Specified Principal-Prepayment Strategy
# 14.5% Interest Rate

### Illustration 2
**Making Three Principal Payments in Advance**

Loan Amount . . . . . . . . . . . . . . $100,000.00
Term . . . . . . . . . . . . . . . . . . . . 30 Years
Total Regular Interest . . . . . . . . . . $340,840.13
Total Regular Interest & Principal . . . $440,840.13

| PMT AMT | PRIN | PMT # | INT | REG BAL |
|---------|------|-------|-----|---------|
| 1,224.56 | 16.22 | 1 | 1,208.33 | 99,983.78 |
| 1,224.56 | (16.42)* | 2 | 1,208.14 | 99,967.36 |
| 1,224.56 | (16.62)* | 3 | 1,207.94 | 99,950.74 |
| 1,224.56 | (16.82)* | 4 | 1,207.74 | 99,933.92** |
| 1,224.56 | 17.02 | 5 | 1,207.53 | 99,916.90 |
| 1,224.56 | 17.23 | 6 | 1,207.33 | 99,899.68 |
| 1,224.56 | 17.43 | 7 | 1,207.12 | 99,882.24 |
| 1,224.56 | 17.65 | 8 | 1,206.91 | 99,864.60 |
| 1,224.56 | 17.86 | 9 | 1,206.70 | 99,846.74 |
| 1,224.56 | 18.07 | 10 | 1,206.48 | 99,828.66 |
| 1,224.56 | 18.29 | 11 | 1,206.26 | 99,810.37 |
| 1,224.56 | 18.51 | 12 | 1,206.04 | 99,791.86 |
| 1,224.56 | 18.74 | 13 | 1,205.82 | 99,773.12 |
| 1,224.56 | 18.96 | 14 | 1,205.59 | 99,754.15 |

*Principal Prepayments
**New Balance

*If three principal prepayments are made every month,*

## Savings with this strategy:
## Interest—$255,181.51   Time—21 yrs. 6 mos.

# Support Information
# The Specified Principal-Prepayment Strategy
# 14.5% Interest Rate

### Illustration 3
**Making Ten Principal Payments in Advance**

Loan Amount . . . . . . . . . . . . . . $100,000.00
Term . . . . . . . . . . . . . . . . . . . 30 Years
Total Regular Interest . . . . . . . . . . $340,840.13
Total Regular Interest & Principal . . . $440,840.13

| PMT AMT | PRIN | PMT # | INT | REG BAL |
|---|---|---|---|---|
| 1,224.56 | 16.22 | 1 | 1,208.33 | 99,983.78 |
| 1,224.56 | (16.42)* | 2 | 1,208.14 | 99,967.36 |
| 1,224.56 | (16.62)* | 3 | 1,207.94 | 99,950.74 |
| 1,224.56 | (16.82)* | 4 | 1,207.74 | 99,933.92 |
| 1,224.56 | (17.02)* | 5 | 1,207.53 | 99,916.90 |
| 1,224.56 | (17.23)* | 6 | 1,207.33 | 99,899.68 |
| 1,224.56 | (17.43)* | 7 | 1,207.12 | 99,882.24 |
| 1,224.56 | (17.65)* | 8 | 1,206.91 | 99,864.60 |
| 1,224.56 | (17.86)* | 9 | 1,206.70 | 99,846.74 |
| 1,224.56 | (18.07)* | 10 | 1,206.48 | 99,828.66 |
| 1,224.56 | (18.29)* | 11 | 1,206.26 | 99,810.37** |
| 1,224.56 | 18.51 | 12 | 1,206.04 | 99,791.86 |
| 1,224.56 | 18.74 | 13 | 1,205.82 | 99,773.12 |
| 1,224.56 | 18.96 | 14 | 1,205.59 | 99,754.15 |

*Principal Prepayments
**New Balance

*If ten principal prepayments are made every month,*

# Savings with this strategy:
# Interest—$310,113.49    Time—27 yrs. 3 mos.

# 7

# The Shorter-Term Strategy

The strategy I am suggesting in this chapter does not apply to existing mortgages. It is for those people who are about to sign a new mortgage. Before you sign a loan of any kind, you should **be aware of all the time options** available to you.

## Ignorance Rules

It seems as if most people do not know they can borrow money on a house **for less than thirty years.** This is evident when you see the disproportionate number of thirty-year loans made by home buyers. I draw this information from personal experience as well as from statistics.

In my early years I was in the home building business in Florida. A great deal of my time was spent in new home sales. As I would help our customers make arrangements for their financing, **almost no one ever asked me about any shorter term for a loan.** They just settled for a thirty-year loan without even inquiring about how much a shorter- term loan would cost per month.

## Lower Interest

A little known advantage of purchasing your home on a shorter term is that many times the bank will **lower your interest rate.** This can amount to as much as one full percentage point or more. The interest rate reduction will vary according to how short a term you are willing to take to repay the loan.

The reason lenders may consider lowering the interest rate on a shorter term loan is obvious. They are locked in to that interest rate for a shorter period of time.

## Five-Year Increments

Shortening the term of a mortgage is usually done in increments of five years. So our illustration will take our standard thirty-year, $100,000 mortgage at 14.5 percent interest, indicating the extra amount you would have to pay to reduce the term to twenty-five years, all the way down to five years. This will also be illustrated with various interest rates.

For instance, if you notice the chart at the end of this chapter, you will see that if you wish to decrease the term of a 14.5 percent mortgage to twenty-five years, you have to add only $17.60 to your payment. If you wish to pay this mortgage off in twenty years, you would have to pay only $55.44 more. At fifteen years, the added payment would be $140.94. If you want to pay off your house in just ten years, you would have to add $358.31. It is possible that you could even pay off the whole house in only five years. To do so, it would take less than twice the payment to cut twenty-five years off your mortgage.

Isn't it surprising how little extra per month it costs to take large periods of time off a thirty-year mortgage?

# Support Information
# The Shorter-Term Strategy

Loan Amount . . . . . $100,000.00

**Number of Years**

| INT | 30 | 25 | 20 | 15 | 10 | 5 |
|-----|------|------|------|------|------|------|
| 14.5% | 1224.56 | 1242.16 | 1280.00 | 1365.50 | 1582.87 | 2352.03 |
| 14.0% | 1184.87 | 1203.76 | 1243.52 | 1331.74 | 1552.66 | 2326.83 |
| 13.5% | 1145.41 | 1165.64 | 1207.37 | 1298.32 | 1522.66 | 2300.98 |
| 13.0% | 1106.20 | 1127.84 | 1171.58 | 1265.24 | 1493.11 | 2275.31 |
| 12.5% | 1067.26 | 1090.35 | 1136.14 | 1223.52 | 1463.76 | 2249.79 |
| 12.0% | 1028.61 | 1053.22 | 1101.09 | 1200.17 | 1434.71 | 2224.44 |
| 11.5% | 990.29 | 1016.47 | 1066.43 | 1168.19 | 1405.95 | 2199.26 |
| 11.0% | 952.32 | 980.11 | 1032.19 | 1136.60 | 1377.50 | 2174.24 |
| 10.5% | 914.74 | 944.18 | 998.38 | 1105.40 | 1349.35 | 2149.39 |
| 10.0% | 877.57 | 908.70 | 965.02 | 1074.61 | 1321.51 | 2124.70 |
| 9.5% | 840.85 | 873.70 | 932.13 | 1044.22 | 1293.98 | 2100.19 |
| 9.0% | 804.62 | 839.20 | 899.73 | 1014.27 | 1266.76 | 2075.84 |
| 8.5% | 768.91 | 805.23 | 867.82 | 984.74 | 1239.86 | 2051.65 |
| 8.0% | 733.76 | 771.82 | 836.44 | 955.65 | 1213.28 | 2027.64 |

This illustration shows the payment needed to reduce the term of the mortgage to the desired number of years.

## Support Information
## The Shorter-Term Strategy
### Loan Amount: $10,000.00
#### Number of Years

This illustration shows the payment needed to reduce the term of the mortgage to the desired number of years.

# 8

# The Lower Interest Rate Strategy

Interest rates take a roller coaster ride through the years. They go up, only to come down again. Because of the tremendous effect interest rates have on the growth of our nation's economy, the government is continually adjusting them up and down. They tend to raise interest rates when inflation climbs, and lower them when the economy threatens to go into recession.

## A Mixed Blessing

This manipulation of the interest rate may benefit the economy, but it is a mixed blessing to the home buyer. During recession when interest rates are lowered, the home buyer enjoys an advantage. However, the person who buys in times of inflation is forced to pay higher interest rates. These rates have gone as high as 15 or 16 percent.

When a person is forced to buy a home with such terribly high interest rates, he should **seek relief from them as soon as possible.** When interest rates go down, he should get out of his high-rate loan into a lower rate.

## Even One Point Is a Big Savings

The difference that just **a one point drop in interest** makes on a thirty-year mortgage **is astronomical.** In the full term of our model 14.5 percent, $100,000 loan, lowering the interest rate by just 1 percent to 13.5 percent will save the borrower $28,506. Just a one point drop in interest can save the borrower over 25 percent of the cost of the original loan. If that same loan can be refinanced at 10.5 percent, the total savings will be $111,513.73. This four point decrease in interest saves more money than was originally borrowed ($100,000). That amounts to a 111 percent savings.

## Keep Making the Old Payment

Now I want to show you the strategy that will cause you to pay off your house even faster. Notice that the payment on your old, high-interest loan will be quite a bit more than the new payment on your lower-interest loan. At 14.5 percent interest, the $100,000 mortgage has a monthly payment of $1,224.56. By lowering the rate to 10.5 percent, the new payment will be only $914.74 per month.

## Don't Give in to Temptation

How tempting it is to just pay that lower payment and pocket the difference. **Don't even think that thought!** Remember, **you are getting out of debt** by rapidly paying off your mortgage. Just plan to keep making the original high payment ($1,224.56) on the new, lower-interest loan. If you do this, you will pay off the mortgage in less than twelve years. With this added strategy, **you will be making regular prepayments** of $309.84 each month.

On the next pages you will see illustrations of mortgages which are moved to a lower interest rate and paid off more rapidly by using the old, higher payment instead of the new monthly payment.

# Support Information
# The Lower Interest Rate Strategy
# 10.5% Interest Rate

Loan Amount . . . . . . . . . $100,000.00
Term . . . . . . . . . . . . . . . 30 Years
Regular Payment . . . . . . . . . $914.74
Total Interest . . . . . . . . . . $76,216.54
Interest + Principal . . . . . . $176,216.54

| 14.5% PMT | PRIN | PMT # | INT | BAL |
|---|---|---|---|---|
| 1,224.56 | 349.56 | 1 | 875.00 | 99,650.44 |
| 1,224.56 | 352.62 | 2 | 871.94 | 99,297.82 |
| 1,224.56 | 355.70 | 3 | 868.86 | 98,942.12 |
| 1,224.56 | 358.82 | 4 | 865.74 | 98,583.30 |
| 1,224.56 | 361.96 | 5 | 862.60 | 98,221.34 |
| 1,224.56 | 365.12 | 6 | 859.44 | 97,856.22 |
| 1,224.56 | 368.32 | 7 | 856.24 | 97,487.90 |
| 1,224.56 | 371.54 | 8 | 853.02 | 97,116.36 |
| 1,224.56 | 374.79 | 9 | 849.77 | 96,741.57 |
| 1,224.56 | 378.07 | 10 | 846.49 | 96,363.50 |
| 1,224.56 | 381.38 | 11 | 843.18 | 95,982.12 |
| 1,224.56 | 384.72 | 12 | 839.84 | 95,597.40 |
| *Payments 13 through 139 omitted to conserve space.* | | | | |
| 1,224.56 | 1,173.37 | 140 | 51.19 | 4,676.95 |
| 1,224.56 | 1,183.62 | 141 | 40.92 | 3,493.31 |
| 1,224.56 | 1,193.99 | 142 | 30.57 | 2,299.32 |
| 1,224.56 | 1,204.44 | 143 | 20.12 | 1,094.88 |
| 1,104.46 | 1,094.88 | 144 | 9.58 | 0.00 |

## Savings with this strategy:
## Interest—$153,088.08    Time—18 yrs.
### Paid With 14.5% Interest Rate Payments

# Support Information
# The Lower Interest Rate Strategy
# 10.5% Interest Rate

Loan Amount . . . . . . . . . $100,000.00
Term . . . . . . . . . . . . . . . 30 Years
Regular Payment . . . . . . . . . $914.74
Total Interest . . . . . . . . . $63,702.39
Interest + Principal . . . . . . $163,702.39

| 14.5% SPLIT PMT | PRIN | PMT # | INT | BAL |
|---|---|---|---|---|
| 612.28 | 208.43 | 1 | 403.85 | 99,791.57 |
| 612.28 | 209.28 | 2 | 403.00 | 99,582.29 |
| 612.28 | 210.12 | 3 | 402.16 | 99,372.17 |
| 612.28 | 210.97 | 4 | 401.31 | 99,161.20 |
| 612.28 | 211.82 | 5 | 400.46 | 98,949.38 |
| 612.28 | 212.68 | 6 | 399.60 | 98,736.70 |
| 612.28 | 213.54 | 7 | 398.74 | 98,523.17 |
| 612.28 | 214.40 | 8 | 397.88 | 98,308.77 |
| 612.28 | 215.26 | 9 | 397.02 | 98,093.51 |
| 612.28 | 216.13 | 10 | 396.15 | 97,877.37 |
| 612.28 | 217.01 | 11 | 395.27 | 97,660.37 |
| 612.28 | 217.88 | 12 | 394.40 | 97,442.48 |
| *Payments 13 through 263 omitted to conserve space.* | | | | |
| 612.28 | 601.60 | 264 | 10.68 | 2,042.16 |
| 612.28 | 604.03 | 265 | 8.25 | 1,438.13 |
| 612.28 | 606.47 | 266 | 5.81 | 831.66 |
| 612.28 | 608.92 | 267 | 3.36 | 222.73 |
| 223.63 | 222.73 | 268 | 0.90 | 0.00 |

## Savings with this strategy:
## Interest—$165,603.75   Time—19 yrs. 9 mos.
### Paid With 14.5% Interest Rate Split Payments

# 9

# Credit Card Strategies

The credit card dilemma of our day is not totally the fault of the borrower. When you realize what has happened in the past, you will better understand why so many people are in such credit card trouble today. The only way to understand how this problem has grown so large is to have a knowledge of the recent history of credit cards.

## The Personal Loan Interview

Not so long ago borrowers were required to go to the bank for **personal interviews before they could be granted a loan.** At this meeting the applicant would be **screened to see if he could afford the payment** the new loan would add to his budget. This seemed to work as a check and balance which kept the majority of the population from borrowing more than they could safely repay.

With the advent of credit cards, a new responsibility was placed on the borrower. It was **now left up to him to decide** whether he was able to afford the purchases he made with them. As the use of credit cards increased, more people began to find themselves in financial problems.

## The Trouble Started Slowly

At first this did not cause nearly so much trouble as it does today. In the early years of credit cards, **the total balance always had to be paid in full** at the end of each month. This kept the borrower's total debt at a level previously established between himself and the lender. However, as the credit card era progressed, there was a new dimension added which brought with it a new set of problems.

# Minimum Payment

The credit card companies added the flexibility of **a minimum payment on the balance,** and two things happened. First, credit card limits were vastly increased. Then installment purchasing without proper credit counseling became commonplace. As credit limits rose from only a few hundred dollars to several thousand, the ever-growing monthly payment became a way of life. This new expanding payment had never before been a part of the average person's budget. Now **impulse items of significant cost could be purchased without any payment planning** on the part of the borrower.

# Pre-Approved Credit Cards

With this new kind of borrowing came the final blow to the good budgeting habits of the average individual. Loan organizations began to issue credit cards to people without knowing their financial condition. For those with fair credit ratings and substantial incomes, **pre-approved cards began to appear** in the mailbox. Some of these cards came just days before the already over-extended recipient would have to begin missing payments on his other cards.

# Borrowing to Make Payments

Today the recipient of these pre-approved cards can borrow against his cash allowance to pay the shortfall of his already overspent paycheck. With this unsound spending, it isn't long until all credit cards are charged to the limit, and bankruptcy becomes the next unavoidable step.

**This doesn't have to happen to you!** Read the following chapter carefully. In it you will find some ideas which may substantially lower your credit card debt.

# 10

# Move Your Debt

Moving your consumer debts to the lowest available interest rate is a simple debt-reduction strategy. It can be accomplished in several ways. It works exceptionally well in the area of credit card debt.

Begin by checking with each of the lending institutions which have issued you credit cards. You will want to know which card charges the lowest annual interest fee. When determining which is the lowest, you should also take into consideration any additional fees charged by that lender such as annual fees, individual transaction fees, and so on.

If you still have unused credit available on the card with the lowest interest rate, transfer the debt from your highest-interest-rate credit card to it. Do this with all your cards until you have transferred as much as possible of your credit card debt to the cards with the lowest interest rates.

## Extend Your Credit Limit

If you have an exceptionally low interest rate on one of your cards, ask the lender to extend your line of credit to allow transference of more, or even all your other credit card debt to it.

I can hear some of you asking, "Do you really think he will do that for me?" Yes, it is possible he will, especially if you promise to cancel all your other credit cards. Another thing which may help motivate him to grant your request is if you agree to move all your banking to his bank. One more thing you can offer him as an incentive is to agree to allow an automatic monthly payment to be withdrawn from your checking account to make the payment.

Please note that many times interest rates are not set in concrete. Even if the banker tells you certain types of loans always cost a certain percentage, try to negotiate. If the lender knows you are comparing his rates with two or three other institutions, he may lower the rate, especially if he knows your checking and savings accounts will go to the bank which extends the desired line of credit. Under the right circumstances, **he may even be willing to reduce the interest rate by a percent or two.**

## Every Little Bit Helps

At first, it may not seem this maneuver will make much difference in your overall credit card debt. But rest assured, it most certainly will. The reason this strategy works so well is because **credit card interest rates can differ as much as 10 percent per year** from the highest to the lowest. If you can effect a 10 percent interest reduction, it can amount to at least $100 per year savings on every $1,000 you owe. Even the reduction of one or two percentage points is a savings to you.

## No-Payment Debt Reduction

Notice the debt reduction from **this strategy takes place without your spending even one penny.** It is a strategy most lenders probably do not want you to know.

If you apply a few strategies like this one, you will quickly begin to take control of your debt. Even if this does not get you out of debt, at least it lets you know **you have a fighting chance!**

## The Key to Rapid Payoff

Once you have successfully moved your credit card debt to the lowest possible interest rate, **be sure you don't make the classic mistake** most people make. Under no circumstances must you allow yourself to pay the lower minimum monthly payment which comes with your new, lower-interest-rate credit card debt. **Keep your monthly payment at least as large as it was before you moved your debt.** When you do, you will find you not only have less total debt to pay because you owe less interest, but you also can make a higher principal payment to more rapidly reduce the debt. Continuing to pay the higher payment causes your restructured credit card debt to pay off much faster.

## Move Your Debts to a Second Mortgage

There is another way to move your debt to a lower interest rate. You can pay off all your bills by placing a new, second mortgage on your home. Today these loans are more commonly known as **home equity loans.**

If you choose to use this strategy, check with the banks and savings and loan associations in your area about this possibility. Remember, if you decide on this course of action, the new loan must be large enough to totally pay off all your outstanding debts.

## Be Sure of a Real Interest Savings

Carefully calculate the interest rate you are presently paying on all your debts. In making this calculation, you must take into consideration the length of time remaining before each of your bills will be paid in full. If you have a low-interest-rate loan that pays off in just a few months, it will tend to give you a false picture of the average interest rate of your present bills. For instance, if your total debt has a four-year payoff, the low interest rate of a short, three-month loan will give you a distorted interest picture.

To properly figure the true interest cost on your present bills, calculate the total dollar amount of the interest you will pay on them if you continue making payments until they are paid in full. Then compare that figure to the total interest you would have to pay for a home equity loan. If the interest expense on the home equity loan is higher than the interest expense on your present bills, it is probably better not to refinance but to stay with the bills you presently have.

## Beware of Variable Interest Rates

There are primarily two types of interest charged on second mortgages, **fixed** and **variable.** A fixed interest rate is one which cannot be raised by the bank during the term of the loan. This is usually the safest form of loan.

With a variable-interest-rate loan, if interest rates rise in your area, they automatically rise on your loan. If interest rates in your area go down, the rate on your mortgage will also go down. There are usually **caps** put on these variable rate loans. A cap sets a maximum amount the interest rate can be raised or lowered. Many times the cap will also set a limit on how much the rate can go up or down within any given year.

## Variable Rates Are Not Always Bad

If a variable-rate second mortgage is the only one available to you, don't give up hope. Under the right circumstances, it can still work for you. For instance, if you are currently paying an average interest rate of 18 percent on all your bills, a 14 percent variable rate with a 2 percent cap might still give you a nice savings. At its worst, the home equity loan could only go up to 16 percent. Even if it does, that is still two full percentage points lower than you are currently paying. If interest rates go down, your rate could go below 14 percent. If it goes down to 12 percent, that would be six percentage points below your old rate.

## Don't Get Stuck by the Point

The smaller the difference between the interest cost of the new loan and the interest cost of your present bills, the more important it becomes to understand the total cost of the new loan. Loan origination fees such as points, document stamps, surveys, attorney's fees, etc., are a real cost in every new mortgage. You must carefully consider whether these costs are within reason before you enter into a home equity loan to consolidate your high-interest debts.

Let me encourage you not to let points scare you off. They are a one-time cost charged on a new loan. There can be times when they are well worth paying if the new loan allows you to move your debt to a substantially lower interest rate. You can automatically save many dollars and years of payments if the new interest rate is significantly lower than the old one.

## Avoid the Credit-Life Trap

Another additional loan cost could be credit life insurance. This is not a benefit to the borrower. Unless you die before the loan is paid in full, it only benefits the lender. Usually there is little or nothing said about this item during the negotiations for the loan. The premium may simply be added to your monthly payment.

If you desire life insurance to pay off your loan in case of your death, you should consider buying a term insurance policy on your own. This can usually be done at a fraction of the cost of credit life. Although your loan officer may want to include this in your note, **it is generally not a requirement.** Leave this clause out of your new loan agreement. If the bank insists you have this coverage as a condition of getting your loan, buy the policy yourself from your own insurance agent or speak with your attorney.

## Watch for Traps

Be nosy! Ask questions, Don't allow the loan officer to intimidate you. Remember, he is getting paid to answer your questions. Boldly continue to ask until you fully understand the exact cost of your new loan. Always keep orderly, legible notes on each loan proposal you receive from each bank or lending institution.

After you have all the figures before you, begin to think of the traps which might be in the best-sounding loan. One of those traps might be that no early payoff is allowed. Maybe there is no cap on the variable rate. It could be that the late payment charges are excessively high. Don't sign until you know exactly what you are signing. Choosing the right loan is not the responsibility of the lender. It is the responsibility of you, the borrower.

## Use the Key to Rapid Payoff

Remember to **never take the new home equity loan at the minimum payment** allowed by the bank. See to it that your new payment is at least **equal to the total of all the payments on the bills you are paying off.** Even if you have only one more month to pay on one of the bills, add it to the total.

In moving your debt, you have made a giant step toward your rapid debt reduction. **Lower interest means that more of your payment goes to pay off the balance of your debt.**

# 11

# Financing an Automobile

In this chapter I would like to share some money-saving suggestions for financing an automobile. When you must purchase a vehicle on time payments, there are several things which can help pay it off much faster than the standard 48 to 60-month loan allows. Consider all of these suggestions carefully. One or more of them might work for you.

## Sell Your Trade-In Yourself

The first rule in any automobile purchase is to always try to sell your present vehicle yourself. You can get as much as 25 percent more than you will get from the dealer. However, **don't attempt to sell your old car after you have bought the new one.** If you don't sell it yourself before your new car purchase, trade it in for whatever the dealer will give you, even if it isn't the full amount you think your car is worth. On the day you purchase your new car, it is much more important to **lower the amount you have to borrow** than to get the most money for your trade-in.

## Early Payoff a Must

When you make financial arrangements to purchase a new automobile, it is important that the lender allows you the **right to prepay the loan.** Don't finance with the automobile manufacturer's credit plan unless they allow you the privilege of periodical early pay downs of the balance **without penalty.** Using the manufacturer's finance plan is usually not recommended because they tend to be **very inflexible.**

Keep in mind that no matter how low the manufacturer's advertised interest rate is, they will usually discount hundreds of dollars off the price of your new car **if you pay them cash.**

## Use All Available Cash

Use all your trade-in money and all the dealer incentive money on your down payment. You should also use as much cash as you can to make the down payment as large as possible. Remember, **every dollar you pay down is a dollar, plus interest, you won't have to pay back.**

## Bank on Good Bank Financing

It is usually best to go to your bank or credit union for your financing. While their interest rate may be a bit higher than the manufacturer's, they tend to be much more flexible. Therefore they will be more eager to tailor-make a loan for you that can be prepaid without penalty or restrictions. Be sure to clearly explain that **it is your purpose to pay off your loan as rapidly as possible.** Insist that your loan allows prepayment. Beware of interest which is not calculated as **simple interest.** Try to avoid loans that require all interest to be paid whether or not you pay off your note early.

## The Down-Payment Blitz

As soon as you decide to borrow money to pay for your car, **declare war on the new loan.** Ask your lender if it is possible for you to borrow the entire amount you plan to finance in **two loans.** Tell him the first one will be a **ninety-day, interest-only loan** for the entire amount of the automobile. Put his mind at ease if he questions your ability to pay off the entire amount in that short length of time. Tell him the first loan (ninety days) is to allow you time for your

**down-payment blitz.** Promise him you will refinance the lower balance into a monthly payment plan at the end of the ninety days.

Now you may still be asking, "Why in the world would I want a ninety-day, interest-only loan?" The reason is simple. This ninety-day period will allow you time to **add as much cash as you can to your down payment.** During this period you should work as much **overtime** as possible, and do whatever you can to raise extra cash, such as having **a garage sale.** This is a time to sell all unnecessary assets in order to make your down payment as large as possible. This can be **a special time when the whole family gets involved** in a ninety-day, pay down marathon. Why, if everyone in the family pitches in, you may be able to lower the amount you have to finance by as much as one-third or even one-half.

## Pay Down the Note As quickly As Possible

Any additional down-payment money you earn during this time should be paid to the bank **the day you get it in hand.** The quicker you repay the ninety-day loan, the lower your overall interest cost will be on that loan. At the end of the ninety days, refinance the remaining balance **for the shortest length of time possible.**

Please keep in mind that these suggestions are subject to the approval of the manufacturer, your dealer, and the lender. Before this debt-reduction plan will work, **you need the cooperation of as many of those who are involved in the purchase as possible.**

# The Best Car Will Become the Worst

There is something important about your automobile that you must keep in mind. No matter how good it is, **it will eventually wear out.** This means you must have a perpetual plan of action to replace your present car. Vehicles tend to wear out or become too expensive to maintain within five or six years. Because of this fact, you must pay off your present car loan as soon as possible. If you take five years (sixty months) to pay off your automobile, just as the car becomes yours, it will be time to buy another one. If you have not made financial provision, **you will have to borrow again to replace it.**

## Pay for Your Next Car Before You Buy It

After finishing your down-payment blitz, try not to take more than thirty months to pay off your automobile loan. Eighteen to twenty months is even more desirable. If you borrow for this shorter length of time, there is a strategic move you can make. When you have made your last payment to the bank, **don't stop making the car payments.**

Yes, you heard me correctly. Don't stop making the payment. I do want you to **stop making your payment to the bank.** You should now **start making the car payment to yourself.** Open a savings account. Begin immediately to make the same monthly payment to yourself that you were paying the bank.

Please consider whether or not you wish to save this money in a regular passbook savings account. You might want to open a money-market account. Check the banks and savings and loan institutions in your area and check with your financial advisor. The amount of interest they pay usually varies greatly on these special, higher-interest-rate accounts.

From the day you start making your monthly payment to your own automobile account, you will find that a wonderful, new thing has happened. Now **the bank is paying the interest on your next car purchase,** instead of you.

## How to Turn $280 Into $10,080

Suppose your car payment is $280 per month. If your loan is paid off in twenty-four months, you can begin setting aside $280, plus the interest the bank pays you each month. If you do this faithfully, it will grow into a substantial amount toward paying for the new car you will need about three years later. With this plan, you should have more than enough saved to **pay cash for your next automobile.**

Please note that, in essence, you are still financing your car on a sixty-month plan. The big difference in this plan and the sixty-month plan of the loan industry is that **you get all the benefits.** On a sixty-month loan with a minimum down payment, you will have to make payments to the bank for almost forty months before you can even sell your car for what you still owe on it. However, if you choose to pay off your loan with the plan I have suggested, using the down-payment blitz and only twenty-four months to pay, you will have a much different result. At the end of forty months, not only will your loan have long since been paid in full, but you will already have accumulated sixteen months of payments toward your next automobile purchase.

# $10,080 Plus an Old Car

Using the monthly payment amount of $280 and the twenty-four month bank note, instead of being at the break-even point at the end of forty months, you will already have saved $3,160 plus its accumulated interest in the bank. If you keep this process up for the remainder of sixty months, you will have saved $10,080 plus interest. With the trade-in price of your old car, you should have enough cash to buy a nicer automobile than the one you trade in.

## Next Time, Buy the Best With Cash

At the time you buy this second automobile for cash, if you continue to save the $280 car payment each month for the following sixty months, when you decide to buy your third automobile, you will have saved $16,800 plus interest. This amount, along with your trade-in, should put you in a position to choose an even better car than the one you purchased before.

By using this rapid debt-reduction strategy when buying an automobile, **driving will be much more fun.**

**John Avanzini** was born in Paramaribo, Surinam, South America, in 1936. He grew up in Texas, and received his doctorate in philosophy from Baptist Christian University, Shreveport, Louisiana. Dr. Avanzini now resides in Fort Worth, Texas, where he and his wife, Patricia, co-pastor **International Faith Center.**

Dr. Avanzini's television program, *Principles of Biblical Economics,* is aired by more than 550 television stations from coast to coast. He speaks nationally and internationally in conferences and seminars every week. His ministry is worldwide, and many of his vibrant teachings are available in tape and book form.

Dr. Avanzini is an extraordinary teacher of the Word of God, bringing forth many of the present truths God is using in these last days to prepare the Body of Christ for His triumphant return.

To share your testimony with John Avanzini, write:

John Avanzini
c/o PLC Department
P.O. Box 917001
Ft. Worth, TX 76117-9001

| QTY | ITEM # | TITLE | COST | TOTAL |
|-----|--------|-------|------|-------|
|  | 1001 | Always Abounding | 6.95 |  |
|  | 1033 | Breakthrough for Prayer | 5.95 |  |
|  | 1007 | Faith Extenders | 8.95 |  |
|  | 1036 | Debt-Free Guarantee | 5.95 |  |
|  | 1009 | Hundredfold | 8.95 |  |
|  | 1027 | It's Not Working | 9.95 |  |
|  | 1028 | John Answers Questions | 6.95 |  |
|  | 1038 | Manifesting Abundance | 5.95 |  |
|  | 1012 | Powerful Principles | 7.95 |  |
|  | 1014 | Stolen Property | 5.95 |  |
|  | 1037 | Better Than Money | 5.95 |  |
|  | 1016 | Wealth of the World | 7.95 |  |
|  | 1003 | War On Debt | 7.95 |  |
|  | 1013 | Rapid Debt-Reduction | 12.95 |  |
|  | 1022 | The Victory Book | 14.95 |  |
|  | 1023 | Have a Good Report | 8.95 |  |
|  |  | Subtotal |  |  |
|  |  | Less 10% Discount |  |  |
|  |  | Shipping & Handling |  | 2.00 |
|  |  | Total Enclosed |  |  |

(___) Enclosed is my check or money order made payable to HIS Publishing Company.

Please charge my: (___) Visa (___) MasterCard
(___) Discover (___) American Express

Account # ☐☐☐☐☐☐☐☐☐☐☐☐☐☐☐

Expiration Date ____/____/____

Signature_____

To assure prompt and accurate delivery of your order, please take the time to print all information neatly.

Name_____

Address_____

City_____State_____Zip_____

Area Code & Phone (_____)_____

Send mail orders to:

**HIS Publishing Company**

**P.O. Box 917001**

**Ft. Worth, TX 76117-9001**

# Trinity Broadcasting Network

*An all-Christian Television Network Broadcasting the*
*Gospel 24 hours a day via Satellite, Cable TV and*
*Local TV Broadcast Stations*

**Alphabetical Directory of TBN Owned and Affiliate Stations**
**(* Indicates an Affiliate-owned station)**

**ALABAMA**
•Berry Ch. 63
•Birmingham Ch. 51
•Decatur Ch. 22
•Dothan Ch. 41
•Florence Ch. 57
•Gadsden Ch. 60
•Huntsville Ch. 67
•Mobile Ch. 21
•Montgomery Ch. 45
•Opelika Ch. 35
Scottsboro Ch. 64
•Selma Ch. 52
•Tuscaloosa Ch. 46
**ALASKA**
•Anchorage Ch. 22
•Anchorage Ch. 41
•North Pole Ch. 4
**ARKANSAS**
•DeQueen Ch. 8
Fayetteville Ch. 42
Ft Smith Ch. 27
•Harrison Ch. 23
•Little Rock Ch. 33
 Mountain Home Ch. 43
**ARIZONA**
Bullhead Ch. 20
Cottonwood Ch. 58
•Duncan Ch. 17
Flagstaff Ch. 62
Globe Ch. 63
•Lake Havasu Ch. 25
Phoenix Ch. 21
Shonto/Tonalea Ch. 38
•Sierra Vista Ch. 33
Tucson Ch. 57
Tucson Ch. 56
**CALIFORNIA**
Alturas Ch. 30
Atwater/Merced Ch. 57

Bakersfield Ch. 55
Chico Ch. 67
Coalinga Ch. 42
•Concord Ch. 42
Desert Hot Springs Ch. 60
•Fresno Ch. 56
•Fresno Ch. 53
•Inyokern/Ridgecrest Ch. 53
Lancaster/Palmdale Ch. 54
•Lompoc Ch. 23
Mariposa Ch. 28
Monterey Ch. 53
•Morro Bay Ch. 22
Palm Springs Ch. 66
Porterville/Visalia Ch. 15
Redding Ch. 65
Sacramento Ch. 69
• Salinas/Santa Cruz Ch. 33
• San Jose/Santa Clara Ch. 22
•San Luis Obispo Ch. 36
Santa Ana Ch. 40
Santa Barbara Ch. 15
•Santa Maria Ch. 65
Ventura Ch. 25
Victorville Ch. 33
**COLORADO**
•Boulder Ch. 17
•Colorado Springs, Ch. 43
Denver Ch. 57
Denver Ch. 66
Denver Ch. 33
•LaJunta Ch. 35
•Lamar Ch. 42
•Las Animas Ch. 40
Loveland Ch. 48
•Pueblo Ch 48
**DELAWARE**
Dover Ch. 67
•Wilmington Ch. 40

**FLORIDA**
•Alachua Ch. 69
Fort Meyers Ch. 67
•Fort Pierce Ch. 21
•Jacksonville Ch. 59
Lake City Ch. 23
•Leesburg/Orlando Ch. 55
•Melbourne Ch. 62
Miami Ch. 45
Sebring Ch. 17
St Petersburg Ch. 60
•Tallahassee Ch. 17
Tampa Ch. 68
West Palm Beach Ch. 47
**GEORGIA**
Albany Ch. 23
Augusta Ch. 65
Brunswick Ch. 33
•Dalton Ch. 23
•Hazelhurst Ch. 63
Marietta Ch. 55
Monroe/Atlanda Ch. 63
Savannah Ch. 67
•Thomasville Ch. 22
Tifton Ch. 20
Valdosta Ch. 66
Waycross Ch. 46
**HAWAII**
•Wailuku
**IOWA**
•Ames Ch. 52
Cedar Rapids Ch. 61
Davenport/Cedar
 Rapids Ch. 58
•Des Moines Ch. 35
•Iowa City Ch. 64
•Keokuk Ch. 60
Ottumwa Ch. 42
•Sioux City Ch. 38
Waterloo Ch. 65

**IDAHO**
Boise Ch. 47
Coeur d' Alene Ch. 53
Pocatello Ch. 15
**ILLINOIS**
•Bloomington Ch. 64
Champaign/Urbana Ch. 34
Decatur Ch. 29
•La Salle Ch. 35
•Marion Ch. 27
Palatine Ch. 36
•Peoria Ch. 41
•Quincy Ch. 16
•Robinson Ch. 57
Rockford Ch. 52
•Sterling Ch. 52
Waukegan Ch. 22
**INDIANA**
•Angola/Ft Wayne Ch. 63
Bloomington Ch. 42
•Clarksville Ch. 26
Elkhart Ch. 67
Evansville Ch. 38
•Fort Wayne Ch. 66
•Jeffersonville Ch. 05
Lafayette Ch. 36
•Muncie Ch. 32
Richmond Ch. 43
Terre Haute Ch. 65
**KANSAS**
Junction City Ch. 25
Manhattan Ch. 31
Salina Ch. 15
Topeks Ch. 21
Wichita Ch. 59
**KENTUCKY**
•Beattyville Ch. 65
Corbin Ch 41
• East Bernstadt Ch. 09
Hopkinsville Ch. 62
•Paducah Ch. 54
**LOUISANNA**
Alexandria Ch. 19
Baton Rouge Ch. 56
•Lake Charles Ch. 51
Mermentau Ch. 45
Monroe Ch. 27
New Iberia Ch. 49
New Orleans Ch. 59
•Opelousas Ch. 62
Shreveport Ch. 65

**MARYLAND**
Cresaptown/
   Cumberlnd. Ch. 16
**MAINE**
Bangor Ch. 17
Danforth Ch. 17
Dover/Foxcroft Ch.19
Farmington Ch. 21
Machias Ch. 21
Madawaska Ch. 17
Medway Ch. 14
•Portland Ch. 18
Presque Isle Ch.51
**MICHIGAN**
Detroit Ch. 66
•Iron Mountain Ch. 08
•Jackson Ch. 59
•Kalamazoo Ch. 24
•Lancing Ch. 69
Muskegon Ch. 29
•Muskegon Ch. 54
•Saginaw Ch. 49
**MINNESOTA**
Duluth Ch. 58
•Fairmont Ch. 28
Minneapolis Ch. 58
Rochester Ch. 60
St Cloud Ch. 19
•Wilmar Ch. 27
**MISSOURI**
•Anderson /Pineville Ch. 09
•Branson Ch. 25
Columbia Ch. 56
•Jeffersonson City Ch. 41
•Joplin/Carthage Ch. 46
•Monett Ch. 38
•Neosho Ch. 32
Poplar Bluff Ch.39
Springfield Ch. 52
St Charles Ch. 34
•St Joseph Ch. 16
•St Louis Ch. 18
**MISSISSIPPI**
**Biloxi Ch. 29**
•Bruce Ch. 07
•Calhoun City Ch. 34
Columbus Ch. 25
•Jackson Ch.64
Mccomb Ch. 36
Meridian Ch. 63
Natchez Ch. 58

Pascagoula Ch. 46
**MONTANA**
•Billings Ch. 14
•Bozeman Ch. 45
Great Falls Ch. 53
Helena Ch. 41
Kalispell Ch. 26
**NORTH CAROLINA**
•Asheville Ch. 69
Charlotte Ch. 68
Fayetteville Ch. 53
•Gastonia Ch. 62
Goldsboro Ch. 59
•Goldsboro Ch. 56
•Greensboro Ch. 61
Greenville Ch. 54
•Hendersonville Ch. 31
Lumberton Ch. 52
Raleigh Ch. 38
Rocky Mount Ch. 53
Statesville Ch. 66
Wilmington Ch. 20
**NORTH DAKOTA**
Fargo Ch. 56
Grand Forks Ch. 22
•Rolette Ch. 20
Williston Ch. 40
**NEBRASKA**
•Council Bluffs/
   Omaha Ch. 45
Lincoln Ch. 39
Ogallala Ch. 26
**NEW JERSEY**
Atlantic City Ch. 36
•Cape May/
   Wildwood Ch. 05
**NEW MEXICO**
•Alamogordo Ch. 29
•Albuquerque Ch. 23
•Carlsbad Ch. 63
•Clovis Ch. 65
•Elida Ch. 36
•Farmington Ch. 47
•Hobbs Ch. 18
Raton Ch. 18
•Roswell Ch. 27
•Roswell Ch. 44
•Roswell Ch. 33
•Ruidoso Ch. 47
**NEVADA**
Carson City Ch. 19

Las Vegas Ch. 57
Reno Ch. 45
**NEW YORK**
Albany Ch. 64
Binghampton Ch. 14
•Buffala Ch. 49
Glens Falls Ch. 14
Jamestown Ch. 10
•Massena Ch. 20
Olean Ch. 22
Poughkeepsie Ch. 54
•Rochester Ch. 59
Utica Ch. 41
**OHIO**
Canton Ch. 17
Chillicothe Ch. 40
•Columbus Ch. 24
Dayton Ch. 68
Deleware Ch. 56
Kirkland/Cleveland Ch. 51
Lexington Ch. 32
• Marietta Ch. 26
•Marion Ch. 39
Portsmouth Ch. 21
•Sandusky Ch. 52
•Seaman Ch. 17
Springfield Ch. 47
•Toledo ( North ) Ch. 68
•Toledo (South ) Ch 46
Youngstown Ch. 39
Zanesville Ch. 36
**OKLAHOMA**
Ardmore Ch. 44
•Balko Ch. 25
•Bartlesville Ch. 17
•Elk City Ch. 52
•Guymon Ch. 53
Lawton Ch. 27
Oklahoma City Ch. 14
•Sayre Ch. 26
•Strong City Ch. 30
**OREGON**
Bend Ch. 33
Coos Bay Ch. 33
•Cottage Grove Ch. 50
•Eugene Ch. 59
Grants Pass Ch. 59
Klamath Falls Ch. 58
Lakeview Ch. Ch. 21
Medford Ch. 57

•Portland Ch. 24
Roseburg Ch. 14
**PENNSYLVANIA**
Erie Ch. 42
•Kingston Ch. 54
Meadville Ch. 52
Pittsburgh, Ch. 65
State College Ch. 42
Williamsport Ch. 39
**SOUTH CAROLINA**
Anderson Ch. 18
Charleston Ch. 44
•Columbia Ch.51
•Greenville Ch. 16
Myrtle Beach Ch. 66
•Myrtle Beach Ch. 43
Orangeburg Ch. 52
**SOUTH DAKOTA**
Aberdeen Ch. 20
Brookings Ch. 15
Huron Ch. 38
Madison Ch. 27
Rapid City Ch. 33
Sioux Falls Ch. 66
Yankton Ch. 31
**TENNESSEE**
Cookeville Ch. 46
Farragut Ch. 66
•Hendersonville Ch. 50
Jackson Ch. 35
•Memphis Ch. 65
•Memphis/HLY Springs
MS Ch.40
Morristown Ch. 31
•Nashville Ch. 36
**TEXAS**
Abilene Ch. 51
•Amarillo Ch. 20
Austin Ch.63
•Beaumont Ch. 34
•Big Spring Ch. 30
Brownwood Ch.26
College Station Ch. 47
•Concord Ch. 12
Corpus Christi Ch. 57
Dallas Ch. 58
•Ft. Stockton
   /Alpine Ch. 30
•Greenville Ch. 53
•Harlingen Ch. 44

•Houston Ch. 14
• Huntsville Ch. 31
•Kerrville Ch. 02
•Killeen Ch. 31
Kingsville Ch. 31
•LaMesa Ch. 47
•Livingston Ch. 66
•Longview Ch. 10
•Lufkin Ch. 05
•Monahans Ch. 28
•Odessa Ch. 42
Palestine Ch. 17
Paris Ch. 42
•Pecos Ch. 64
San Angelo Ch. 19
San Antonio Ch.33
San Antonio Ch. 20
•Snyder Ch. 26
•Texarkana Ch. 30
•Tyler Ch. 20
Victoria Ch. 43
•Wichita Falls Ch. 26
**UTAH**
Ogden Ch. 64
•Salt Lake City Ch.36
Salt Lake City KTBN Rad.
Vernal Ch. 39
**VIRGINIA**
•Danville Ch. 18
•Front Royal/Winchstr Ch.
28
•Harrisonburg Ch24
Lynchburg Ch. 32
Roanoke Ch. 49
•Winchester Ch. 48
•Woodstock Ch. 10
**VERMONT**
Burlington Ch. 16
**WASHINGTON**
Aberdeen Ch. 23
Ellensburg Ch. 39
•Longview Ch. 36
•Richland Ch. 49
Spokane Ch. 55
Tacoma/Seattle Ch. 20
•Wenatchee Ch. 13
•Wenatchee Ch. 59
•Yakima Ch. 64
**WISCONSIN**
Green Bay Ch.68

Janesville Ch. 19
•La Crosse Ch. 44
Madison Ch. 33
Oshkosh Ch. 34
Ripon Ch. 42
Sheboygan Ch. 20
Waupaca Ch.55
**WEST VIRGINIA**
•Charleston Ch. 45
•Huntington Ch. 19
Parkersburg Ch. 39
**WYOMING**
•Casper Ch. 13
Green River Ch. 35

# INTERNATIONAL STATIONS

## CENTRAL AMERICA

**BELIZE**
Belize City Ch. 23
**COSTA RICA**
St. Jose Ch. 23
Santa Elena Ch. 53
Cerro De La Muerte Ch. 53
Limon Ch. 23
Zapotal Ch 53
**EL SALVADOR**
El Salvador Ch. 25
**HONDURAS**
Tegulcigalpa Ch. 57
**NICARAGUA**
Managua Ch. 21
Eslteli Ch. 25
LaGateda Ch. 27 (under
    const.)

## SOUTH AMERICA
**ARGENTINA**
Buenas Aires Ch. 68

**BOLIVIA**
LaPas Ch. 27
**BRAZIL**
Manaus Ch. 8
Porto Velho Ch. 6

**CHILE**
Santiago Ch. 50
**COLUMBIA**
Cali
**ECUADOR**
Quito Ch. 27
Guayaquil Ch 28

## AFRICA
**BOPHUTHATSWANA**
**CISKEI, SA**
•Bisho Ch. 24
**LESOTHO, SA**
•Maseru
**NAMIBIA, SA**
Windhoek
**TRANSKEI, SA**
•Umata Ch. 67
Butterworth Ch. 25
Mt. Ayliff Ch. 27
Ikwezi/Ngangelizwe Ch. 51
Queenstown Ch. 10
Port. St. Johns Ch. 65
Engcoro Ch. 49 (under
    const.)
Mount Fletcher Ch. 51
    (under const.)
## REPUBLIC OF SOUTH AFRICA
•TV 1 Channel 13
•TV 2 Channel 9
**SWAZILAND**
•Mbabane
**ZAMBIA**
Lukasa
## SOUTH PACIFIC
**KINGDOM OF TONGA**
Nuku-Alofa A3M Ch. 7
## EUROPE
**ALBANIA**
Various Government-
owned Channels


**ICELAND**
Reykjavik Ch. 53 and 45


**ITALY**
**Lombardia Region**
Agno Magnaso Ch. 39
Biella Ch. 59

Campione Ch. 44
Como, Ch. 28
Ivrea Ch. 36
Maccaagno Ch. 45
Milano Ch. 11
Pavia Certosa Ch. H1
Porto Ceresio Ch. 468
Valdosta Ch. 28
Varese Ch. 33
Viggiu Ch. 46

**Piemonte Region**
Torre Bert Ch. 60
Piazza Lancia Ch. 10
Pecetto Torino Ch. 27
LaMorra Ch. 60
Guarene Ch. 28
Azzano Ch. 29
St. Stafano Ch. 48
Mombaruzzo Ch. 68
Bricco Olio Ch. H2
Monte Ronzone Ch. 29
Corio Ch. 60
Nieve Ch. 42
Canale Ch. 26
Dogliani Ch. 21
Somano Ch. 42
Paroldo Ch. 42
St. Michele Mondovi Ch. 68
Alba Bricco Capre Ch. 68

**Lazio Region**
Rome Ch. 33
Rome/Mt. Cavo Ch. 47
P. Nibbio Ch. 64
Mt.. Calcarone Ch. 50
Mt. Artemisio Ch. 35
Rocca d'Arce Ch. 47
Fumone Ch. 39
Arpino Ch. 48
Valle Maio Ch. 61
Rocca Monfina Ch. 50
Mt. Orlando Ch. 48
Avezzano Ch. 31
Mt. Cicoli Ch. 42
Segni Ch. 34
Vicalvi Ch. 63
Montattico Ch. 53
Capistrello Ch. 29
Civita d'Antino Ch. 673
Meta Ch. 58
Isola Liri Ch. 24
Subiaco Ch. 22
Gadamello Ch. 26
Mt. Amita, Ch. 47
Mt. Paradiso Ch. 61
Scansano Ch. 54

Mt. St. Biagio Ch. 57
St. di Fondi Ch. 24
St. Felice Circeo, Ch. 43
Secca Volsci Ch. 49
St. Vito Romano Ch. 44
Castro Volsci Ch. 31
St. Incarico Ch. 41
Itri Ch. 24
Balsorano Ch. 35
Pesche Ch. 58

**GREECE**
Athens Ch. 62
Corinth Ch. 54
Macedonia Ch. 62

**SWITZERLAND**
Locarno Ch. 37

**RUSSIA**
St. Petersburg Ch. 40
Moscow Ch. 3

**CARIBBEAN**
**GRAND CAYMAN**
Grand Cayman Ch. 21

**GRENADA**
St. George's Ch. 13

**HAITI**
Port-Au-Prince Ch. 16

**NEVIS**
Charlestown Ch. 13

**ST. LUCIA**
Castries Ch. 13

**TBN**
**SHORTWAVE RADIO**

**KTBN SUPERPOWER**
**SHORTWAVE RADIO**
St. Lake City, Utah
8 AM - 4 PM (PST)
15.590 MHGz.
4 PM - 8 AM (PST)
7.510 MHz
*(Reaching Around
the World)*

RADIO PARADISE
ST. KITTS, W.I.
830 KHz AM Radio
24 Hours a Day

For more information call or write:

# Trinity Broadcasting Network
PO Box A
Santa Ana, CA 92711
**24-Hour Prayer Line**
*(714) 731-1000*

**E-Mail Address**
tbntalk@tbn.org
**TBN Web Site**
http://www.tbn.org

**TDD Phone Line**
(714) 832-7071
(For Deaf & Hearing
Impaired <u>only</u>)